Savoring Slidell

Its Saucy People, Spicy Recipes & Southern Scenery

Camellia Watercolor by Lucy Band

Published by the Slidell Garden Club
in Association with

books à la carte

A Division of the Publishing Resources Group, Inc.
www.booksalacarte.com • www.pubresgroup.com

Special Thanks to the Slidell Garden
Club Book Publishing Committee:

Kathryn Jones, Chair
Lucy M. Band
Jan Brown
Charlotte Elias
Catherine Walker

Savoring Slidell

COVER PHOTO *BAYOU LIBERTY RISING*
BY CHARLOTTE LOWRY COLLINS

EIGHT A.M ALL ABOARD – CRESCENT CITY TO POINTS NORTHEAST—SLIDELL TRAIN DEPOT
OIL BY LEN HEATHERLY

Library of Congress Control Number: 2012900056

by the Slidell Garden Club founded 1959

SAVORING SLIDELL—*its saucy people, savory recipes, and southern scenery*

SAVORING SLIDELL documents Slidell's colorful history, its lush landscapes, its stunning regional art and its traditional, local cuisine.

Copyright © 2012 by Books *á la Carte* an imprint of the Publishing Resources Group

ISBN 978-09-8471452-0 (hardback : alk. paper)

Printed in South Korea by PACOM

These companies, institutions and families have contributed to make the production of this book possible. They have our profound thanks for their support and their civic pride.

Omni Pinnacle, LLC

Garden Spot Nursery

Northshore Harbor Center

Slidell Memorial Hospital

Cajun Encounters

JOY Lutheran Bible Study

Ochsner Northshore Hospital

Tammany Holding Co, LLC

Kathryn B. Jones

Ellermann Family

Dr. and Mrs. Russ Westfall

Jan Smith Stumph

Ozone Camellia Club

Lishman's City Market

Dedication—The women of the Slidell Garden Club dedicate this book "to the people of Slidell: those who came before us, those who are with us now, and those who will come after us to continue our work."

Savoring Slidell

Its Saucy People, Spicy Recipes & Southern Scenery

TABLE OF CONTENTS

FOREWORD 5

WELCOME TO SLIDELL 6
Growing Up in the Big House 6
John Besh: Slidell Son Talks of Home and Food . . . 8
Slidell, The Man 10
Slidell, The Town 11
Early Industry 12
Early Families 14
Early Churches 16

GONE BUT NOT FORGOTTEN 17
St. Christopher's Curve Inn 17
The Streets of Slidell 18
Politics As Unusual 20
The "Sleepy" Village 20
Early Schools 22
Historic Landmarks 23
Living The American Dream 24
Footprints on our hearts 26

SLIDELL, THE CAMELLIA CITY 28
Mayor Freddy Drennan 29
NASA 30
The Reine Family 32
Langiappe 37
Dynamic Duo 38
JOY Bible Study 39
Northlake Oral and Maxillofacial Surgery 40
Le Cotillion 41
Slidell Little Theatre 42
Ozone Camellia Club 43

The Human Touch 44
Junior Auxilliary 45
Lions Club 45
Slidell Women's Civic Club 46
Rotary Club 46
Honoring our Service Heroes 47
Celebrating Families 48
Celebrating Traditions 49
Mardi Gras 50
Christmas 51
Destruction 54
Reconstruction 55

BAYOU BONFOUCA 56
Bayou Bonfouca 58
Langiappe 65
Antique Alley 67
Community Parks 68
Sports and Community 69
The Slidell Garden Club 70
Garden Spot Nursery 71
Slidell Memorial Hospital 72

BAYOU LIBERTY 74
Rooted In Liberté 76
Shell Midden 77
St. Genevieve's Church 78
Doucette Family 79
A Creole Cottage 80
Francois Cousin Home 81
Tranquility Plantation 82

Gardner and Ronnie Kole 83
Camp Salmen 84
Pirogue Races 86
All Saints Day 88
First you make a roux 92
Two Grand Ladies of Bayou Liberty 95
George B. Dunbar 96

LAKE PONTCHARTRAIN 98
Pontchartrain's Pride 100
Northshore Harbor Center 102
Tammany Holding Company, llc 104
Lishman City Market 106
Shrimp Boats is a' Comin' 110
Banks of Pontchartrain 114
Preservation and Restoration 116

THE WEST PEARL 118
Entering the West Pearl 120
Cajun Encounters 122
Ochsner Medical Center – North Shore 124
Backyard Living at its Best 126
Fish Fry Festivities 128
Indian Village 135
The Front Porch Swing 140
Larger than Life 141
Leaving the West Pearl 142

SPECIAL THANKS 144

FOREWORD

With their saucy charm and spicy food, the people of Slidell, Louisiana, cordially welcome you to their city and its natural beauty, rich history, and southern ambience. This book celebrates the lifestyle its residents cherish. They invite you to travel the bayous and back roads. You'll glimpse its past, visit its present and glance at what the future may hold.

Settle down with a café au lait and take a tour of this scenic city, via its waterways: Bayou Bonfouca, Bayou Liberty, West Pearl River, and Lake Pontchartrain. Seen from its waters, you'll visit places tucked away from the highways and the three interstates which intersect there. These waterways, the wildlife, and the nature preserves, set the scene for a peaceful lifestyle many only dream of living.

The area is dotted with majestic old homes, impressive new ones and magnificent gardens.

The people of Slidell enjoy the big city excitement of New Orleans, only 30 miles south, and the gentle leisure of the Gulf Coast, only 30 miles east. They, and their city, embrace the best of both worlds.

The women of the Slidell Garden Club, who created this book, have worked for more than 50 years to enhance the beauty of this, the Camellia City. Many of them represent families who have been here for generations, laying the foundation from which Slidell has flourished with Southern charm and dignity.

From these pages you'll get a taste of the city, seasoned by its gracious past and flavored by its businesses, craftsmen, and community leaders. There are recipes for your kitchen, hints for your garden, and art for your mind and soul to savor.

Welcome home. Sit and stay awhile.

CAMELLIA
OIL BY MARY CHRISTOPHER

Welcome to Slidell

Growing Up in the Big House at 127 Cleveland Avenue

One of the most beautiful landmarks in Slidell is the Salmen-Fritchie House. Built in 1895 for the Fritz Salmen family, it stands proudly on three acres on the corner of Front Street and Cleveland Avenue.

Homer G. Fritchie, Sr., moved his family into the 6500 square foot grand home in 1939. The family included his wife, Nellie Bousquet Fritchie; their children, Nelouise "Suzy" Fritchie Williams (named for her mother and grandmother Louise), Barbara Fritchie Ware, Beth Fritchie Dendinger, Homer, Jr., and Grace Fritchie Burkes.

Grace Burkes, smiles as she recalls wonderful memories of her childhood in the Fritchie home, which also included three grandparents (Momie, Mamaw and PaPa Bousquet) and Cousin Grace.

"Thank goodness the house had nine bedrooms and five baths!" she laughed. Six bedrooms and four baths were on the ground floor off the great hall with its 12-foot ceilings and running 70 feet from the front porch to the formal dining room. At the rear of the house was the oversized kitchen, large breakfast room and a back porch.

"The sun parlor, where we all had many parties, was between one bedroom and the "porte-cachere," the carport. "We'd sunbathe on the roof of the porte-cachere and play ping pong on the front porch with its hammock and wicker rocking chairs."

The great hall's impressive staircase leads to a mezzanine floor, then up a few steps to the massive pool room, "We all loved playing pool and balls occasionally jumped the table and landed on the floor." Upstairs there were three bedrooms and one bath.

"The attic space was intriguing and we spent many hours investigating the place. Of course when we came back down the grand staircase, some of us attempted to slide down the banister until Mother made it off limits." The main floor had steam heat radiators. "At five o'clock in the morning, Dad would go down to the boiler room, near the wine cellar, and bang on a pipe to fire up the heat. Then the clanging began and soon the home was warm as toast."

The home's rose garden eventually became a camellia garden. "There were massive oak trees and 17 pecan trees. We helped pick up the pecans so my father could crack and peel them. My mother would make pralines at Thanksgiving and Christmas.

"The front yard had yellow day lilies and palm trees. (We used the palms on Palm Sunday.) The tandem garage was next to an artesian well that filled a shallow pool and a gold fish pond (great places to swim!). A wash shed (between the garage and the barn) was close to a magnificent oak with a huge wisteria vine (large enough to swing on --- which of course, we did). Jane and Tarzan would have been envious."

Grace continued, "Behind the barn was an old chicken coop. We loved to jump from the loft of the barn to the top of the coop. There was also a playhouse near the barn. My father had a Victory Garden with vegetables and fig trees in abundance. Mother was a great cook; so, we all enjoyed the harvest."

It's obvious; the "Big House" was a great place to grow up. "When each of his four daughters was to be married, my father offered the wedding or money.

"Poor Mother and Dad --- we all took the wedding and had the receptions at the house! When I look back on our early years, I realize Mother and Dad were saints and they made the Big House a wonderful family home."

Salmen-Fritchie Home Courtesy of
Grace Fritchie Burkes

John Besh: Slidell Son Talks of Home and Food

One of the nation's most acclaimed chefs is Slidell's John Besh. His six restaurants in the New Orleans area, including La Provence near Slidell, have earned him kudos for his dedication to local flavors and creation of culinary masterpieces.

In addition to his business responsibilities, Besh donates much of his time to philanthropic work. Through his partnership with an emergency reconstruction firm, Besh provides high quality ready-to-eat meals for emergency response teams throughout the United States and around the world. Slidellians are very proud of this native son.

"Growing up in Slidell was an amazing experience that I would not trade for the world," Besh notes. "It instilled in me a sense of family…and a love of food." He adds, "We, in this area, are so lucky to be surrounded by lakes and rivers to fish and land to hunt."

As a child he hunted, fished and cooked with his father and grandfather and he makes the time in his hectic schedule to do the same with his four sons. "Slidell will always be a treasure in my heart and I am sure my family will look back on growing up here with fond memories."

JOHN BESH MAKES HIS DELICIOUS SHRIMP, CHICKEN, AND ANDOUILLE JAMBALAYA FOR HIS FAMILY AT HOME AND SHARES THE RECIPE ON THE FOLLOWING PAGE.

Shrimp, Chicken and Andouille Jambalaya

Ingredients:

3 Lb Andouille sausage, diced

2 Lb fresh pork sausage, removed from casings

2 Lb bacon, diced

8 skinless/boneless chicken thighs, cut roughly into 1 inch cubes

5 Lb Louisiana white shrimp, peeled and de-veined

6 large onions, diced

4 bell peppers, diced

10 stalks celery, diced

12 cloves garlic, minced

9 cups converted Louisiana white rice

6 cups crushed tomatoes

6 cups rich chicken broth

2 tsp. dried thyme

2 dried bay leaf

3 tbs. pimenton de la vera (Spanish smoked paprika)

2 tbs. cayenne pepper

2 tbs. salt

1 tbs. black pepper

1 tbs. celery salt

3 bunches green onions, chopped

Method:

First of all, try to use a large (3-5 gallon) "seasoned" cast iron pot if you can. If not, find the heaviest iron/ enamel pot that you can get your hands on. It's well worth the investment for many of these one-pot recipes that we love cooking down here.

Next, you are going to want to heat the pot over a high flame until it becomes moderately hot before reducing the flame to medium. What this will do is allow the pot to heat uniformly, preventing "hot spots" or little areas that may be more prone to burning than other areas.

Once hot, start by rendering the bacon and sausages, while stirring slowly over medium heat. While the pork is rendering, go ahead and season the chicken thighs with salt and black pepper. Add the chicken to the pot and continue to stir intermittenty. Cook the chicken until it becomes golden brown in color.

After the chicken has browned add the onions to the pot and allow them to brown as well, prior to adding the bell peppers, garlic and celery. Be sure to continue stiring from time to time in an effort that will ensure everything in the pot cooks evenly. Next add the rice and remaining dry ingredients to the pot while stirring frequently for the next 3 minutes. Raise the heat to high once again and add the tomatoes and chicken stock to the pot. Bring the liquid to a boil before reducing the heat to medium/low and covering the pot for 15 minutes.

While the rice is cooking in the covered pot, season the shrimp with salt and pepper and reserve along with the green onions to be added in a moment.

After the rice has simmered for 15 minutes go ahead, remove the lid from the pot and fold in the shrimp and green onions. Turn the heat off and cover the pot again for an additional 10 minutes.

Remove the lid, fluff the jambalaya and serve!

SLIDELL, THE MAN

To understand how the City of Slidell got its name, one must take a short review of the city's history. Because the area was the first high ground north of Lake Pontchartrain, the New Orleans and Northeastern Railroad needed a railroad station there.

The railroad's banking syndicate was headed by Baron Emile Erlanger. It was Baron Erlanger who chose the name "Slidell" to honor his father-in-law, John Slidell. Although John Slidell had never been to the city, Baron Erlanger wanted John Slidell to be remembered for his service to Louisiana, the United States and the Confederacy.

John Slidell was born in New York City in 1793, graduated from Columbia, was admitted to the bar and moved to New Orleans in 1819 to practice law.

Geri U. Staines wrote in the Slidell Centennial Souvenir Brochure that one of the highlights of Slidell's life was his romance with Marie Mathilde Deslonde, the daughter of a wealthy plantation owner in Belle Pointe, Louisiana. Staines notes: "Through his association with Marie Mathilde, he became friendly with her prosperous Creole family, whose estate included one of the grandest mansions of the time. He and Marie married and "he was to share not only in the affluence of his in-laws, but also in their social prominence." They had five children, including his daughter, Mathilde, who married Baron Erlanger.

He was a member of the Louisiana House of Representatives, the United States House of Representatives and the Senate. He resigned from Congress when Louisiana seceded from the Union and was appointed the Confederate Commissioner to France charged with seeking aid from England and France.

His wife died while they were in England. Slidell was denied permission to return to the United States and died in exile at Cowes, England, in 1871. He was interred in a private cemetery near Paris.

SLIDELL, THE TOWN

From its incorporation in 1888 until 1960, Slidell was a typical, sleepy Southern town. The natural resources of the area provided industry for its people. They opened stores, built churches, schools and a few saloons.

As most towns do, Slidell has its share of folk heroes, stories and secrets. The native Indians, the people from across the lake, and those from across the oceans converged to make Slidell a unique melting pot of cultures.

As you travel back in time through the next few pages and sample our history, memories will be stirred and curiosity awakened.

A more detailed history of Slidell is available from GOSH (Guardians of Slidell History) and the Slidell Museum, along with publications by Charles J. Fritchie, Jr. and Dan A. Ellis.

TEMPTING LIPS
PORCELAIN BY SALENAH COOPER

Jezebel Sauce

1 (10-ounce) jar pineapple preserves
1 (10-ounce) jar apple jelly
3 ounces bottled horseradish
1 1/2 ounces dry mustard
1 teaspoon coarse ground black pepper

Mix all ingredients well. Chill and allow flavors to meld.

Serve with wild game, barbeque, ham or any meat of choice. It also makes a good appetizer by spooning it over a block of cream cheese and serving with assorted crackers.

Creole Tomato and Onion Tart

1 unbaked 10-inch fluted tart shell
3 tablespoons olive oil
3 medium-size sweet onions, thinly sliced
2-3 medium-size Creole tomatoes, thinly sliced
1 cup grated Gruyere cheese
 Salt and freshly ground black pepper to taste

Preheat oven to 400 degrees. Place tart shell in 10-inch tart pan with removable bottom and press gently against the bottom and sides. Trim any excess pastry and set dish aside.

Heat olive oil in a skillet over medium heat. Add onions and sugar; cover and cook, stirring occasionally, until onions are golden and slightly caramelized, about 10 minutes. Remove and set aside to cool.

Spread cooled onion mixture into the bottom of the tart shell. Arrange tomatoes over onions and sprinkle evenly with cheese. Season with salt and pepper to taste.

Bake until cheese is melted and golden, 25 to 30 minutes. Remove from oven and allow to rest a few minutes before cutting to serve.

EARLY INDUSTRY

CANULETTE SHIPBUILDING COMPANY, COURTESY OF BRUCE CANULETTE

Slidell's natural resources contributed to her emergence as an industrial center, most notably her forests, her clay and her deep, calm waterways.

The pine forests produced lumber for the building of naval vessels. Also, by-products of the pine (tar, pitch, and turpentine) were an industry of its own. Cypress lumber and other hardwoods were used for building material. The natural waterways made it easy to load and transport goods. The area clay, used by Native Americans for centuries, was excellent for bricks and pottery.

Fritz Salmen emigrated from Switzerland to Gulfport, Mississippi. Shortly after the railroad was constructed, he moved to

Slidell. He established a brickyard between the Railroad and Bayou Bonfouca, using clay from the area now known as Palm Lake. His younger brothers, Jacob and Albert joined him and added a sawmill and, in the 1880s, a small shipyard named Salmen Shipyard.

It became Slidell Shipbuilding Company in 1914 when the Salmen brothers, with Andrew D. Canulette, formed a stock company and renamed it. The principal owners were the Canulette family, and in 1919, it became Canulette Shipbuilding. Andrew and his son, Frank, and Frank's son, Mayo, all served as presidents of the company.

In its lifetime, the shipyard constructed and repaired large ocean-going vessels, tugboats, barges and ships and made major contributions in both world wars. Sold in 1954, it was renamed J&S Shipbuilding; and, sold again in 1957, was renamed Southern Shipbuilding.

In its heyday, the shipyard employed as many as 1900 men and women. The whistles at shift changing time and the lines of cars crossing Bayou Bonfouca to go to work, were a familiar part of everyday life in Slidell.

In 1993, the shipyard was closed and razed; its employees gone and its whistle silenced. The Canulette family, however, remains an integral part of the Slidell community. Prominent in the business community and city government (most notably Pat Canulette who served as sheriff of St. Tammany Parish from 1980-1996), their commitment to the community endures.

As already noted, brick making was a mainstay of Slidell's economy. The largest was the Salmen Brick and Lumber Company, established by Fritz Salmen in the 1880s. In the 1890s it supplied over a million bricks for buildings in New Orleans, including the St. Charles, Desoto, Grunewald Hotels and Maison Blanche and D H Holmes Department stores.

Colonel P.W. Schneider acquired St. Joe Bricks in 1891. Still in business today, it is the oldest family brick manufacturer east of the Mississippi and is operated by Peter "Pete" Schneider III, a descendant of the colonel. The Schneiders bought the Salmen brickyard in 1931 and operated it until about 1960.

German Apple Cake

8	tablespoons unsalted butter, softened
3	large eggs, separated
1	lemon, zested and juiced
1	cup all-purpose flour
	Pinch of salt
3/4	teaspoon baking powder
1	cup sugar
4-6	apples, peeled, cored and thinly sliced
	Confectioner's sugar, for topping

Preheat oven to 350 degrees.

Butter a 9 x 9-inch baking dish and set aside.

In a large bowl of electric mixer, cream butter and sugar until fluffy. Add egg yolks, lemon zest and juice and continue mixing until smooth. Sift together flour, salt, baking powder and sugar and add to the mixture, blending well.

Meanwhile, beat egg whites until stiff. Carefully fold into cake mixture and pour into the prepared pan.

Arrange apple slices on top, core-side down. Do not space slices too far apart or cake will rise between slices.

Bake for about 45 minutes. Test for doneness by inserting a sharp knife in the center of the cake, being sure it comes out clean.

When cake is cool, dust lightly with confectioner's sugar.

Early Families

The Guzman Family

The Guzman family acquired a Spanish Land Grant in 1859. These 4400 acres stretched from Lake Pontchartrain to Bayou Patassat and the east bank of Bayou Bonfouca, where Slidell eventually grew. At one time, Pontchartrain Boulevard was called Guzman Road. John Guzman, who operated a small brickworks and a ferry near modern Bayou Liberty Road, ceded right of way to the railroad through his land and sold other property to Fritz Salmen, who developed Slidell's first significant industry, a mechanized brickyard.

PHOTO OF THE GUZMAN FAMILY TAKEN ABOUT 1915. BACK ROW — CHARLES PIERRE NUNEZ, ELLA GUZMAN NUNEZ, FLORENCE GUZMAN, WILLARD MOORE HOLDING CHARLES (CALLED CHILI). MIDDLE ROW — DEG GUZMAN, AMELIA GUZMAN (CALLED BOB), BUSTER GUZMAN, MOLLY GUZMAN MOORE HOLDING SON, JOHN MOORE. STANDING IN FRONT OF MOLLIE IS ARTEMISE GUZMAN (CALLED MESIE). FRONT ROW — CHARLES VALERIE GUZMAN, HOLDING SON BILLY, MARIE GUZMAN, MOLLY CROCKETT, WHITMIRE SADLER (MOTHER OF SALLIE), CARY GUZMAN, SALLIE WHITMIRE GUZMAN (WIFE OF CHARLES) HOLDING SON, JOHN BARRY. PHOTO COURTESY OF ELLEN LAMARQUE.

The Haddad Family

In 1908 Philip Haddad, Sr., came to Slidell as an apprentice in shoemaking. After five years he realized that handmade shoes did not have a market in Slidell to meet the needs of his seven children and wife. He opened a clothing store, The Leader Department Store, and began a business that lasted for 50 years.

Even with his large family and business obligations, Haddad found time to serve his community. Active with the Boy Scouts and Red Cross, he was also president of the Slidell Lion's Club and president and charter member of the Bayou Vincent Golf Club. He served his church in many ways and was known for the turkeys he gave away each Thanksgiving.

A month after celebrating his 70th birthday and 50th business anniversary,

MARIE G. HADDAD, PHILIP N. HADDAD SR., VIOLET H. MOORE, JEANETTE H. MCDANIEL, ADELE H. OWENS, NELL H. PARKER, PHILIP N. HADDAD JR. NEBEHA H. BROOM, ELIZABETH H. FOGG.   PHOTO COURTESY OF CAROL BROOM FACIANE

he died while on a visit to Lebanon. His children, who inherited his business acumen and love of Slidell, continued to serve Slidell in the business community, and the community-at-large, as do their children. McDaniel's Clothing (Jeanette Haddad McDaniel), Haas's 5 and Dime (Philip Haddad) and House of Beauty, originally Haddad's Beauty Shop (Nebeha Haddad Broom and Liz Haddad Fogg), are a few of the many contributions this family made to the community. The grandchildren now follow in the footsteps of their grandfather.

The Mire Family

In the early 1900s Julius A. Mire graduated from bookkeeping school and moved to Slidell to work for the Schneider Brick Company. Later he became an accountant for Neuhauser's Department Store. With his experience and the help of a friend, Mamie Powers, he then started his own business, Mire's Hardware Store. He married Janie Canulette. Their son, Julius "Shine" Mire continued the family business. His wife, Ethel, and their seven children all helped in the store.

Mire's Hardware Store was the place to go for everyday hardware, hard to find items and to visit with neighbors. Many people called the store Noah's Ark because it was reputed to have two of EVERYTHING. The Mire's legacy continues today. Drew Mire (fourth generation with three Mire boys of his own) eulogized his dad, Johnny Mire, former principal of Slidell Junior High. He spoke of Johnny Mire's courageous battle with cancer, his faith, and his love of family and community. He honored him as an individual and also as a Mire, the family who has contributed to the Slidell community for over a century.

EARLY CHURCHES

ABOVE, A SKETCH OF 1ST UNITED METHODIST CHURCH AS IT IS REMEMBERED IN ITS LOCATION FROM 1906-1961.

According to Charles Fritchie, author of *Notes on Slidell History* and founding member of Guardians of Slidell History (GOSH), "White Methodist, Baptist, Catholic and Presbyterian congregations and churches, as well as an African Methodist Episcopal (AME) church and the African-American Starlight Baptist church all were established between approximately 1885 and 1900.

The original sites and structures of many of the churches have changed due to natural disasters such as fire and water and the natural growth of the congregations. Since its beginning Slidell has been a town of profound faith that expresses itself in many and varied congregations and religions.

PHOTO BY GILDA PERKINS

Gone but not Forgotten

St. Christopher's Curve Inn

St. Christopher's Curve Inn, located where Pontchartrain Drive curved to Front Street and known for their roast beef po-boys with red gravy, was a favorite of locals and those traveling from New Orleans to Mississippi.

THE STREETS OF SLIDELL

FREMAUX (free-mow)– Born Napoleon Joseph Fremaux, he changed his name to Leon. He was an engineer, who assisted with the railroad construction, and a New Orleans surveyor. Fremaux designed the layout of the town of Slidell.

ERLANGER—Baron Frederick Erlanger was the head of the banking syndicate which financed the railway. It was Erlanger who named the town "Slidell" in honor of his wife's father.

BOUSCAREN—G. Bouscaren was the chief engineering officer of the railroad.

COUSIN (coo-san)—Armand Cousin was the head of a locally prominent family from the Bayou Liberty area.

GUZMAN—John Gusman owned large tracts of land in the Slidell area before it was a town. He sold several parcels to the railroad.

ROBERT (row-bear)—St. Pierre Thomas Robert, along with Guzman, owned large tracts of land on which Slidell sits today.

CAREY STREET—Named for Mary Ann Carey, who married John Guzman.

SGT. ALFRED DRIVE—Formerly Third Street, was named for Sgt. Earl Alfred, the first Slidell policeman to be killed in the line of duty.

GAUSE BOULEVARD—Named for George H. Gause.

APPLE PIE RIDGE ROAD—Derived its name from soldiers traveling on Military Road who would stop to eat Mrs. Taylor's delicious pies. The descendents of the Taylor family still live in the area today.

PICTURED ARE (FROM LEFT) JOE JOHNSON, DALE TIDRICK, AND ROBERT RUGAN.
PHOTO BY GILDA PERKINS

Snippet from the Past

PRIVATE GEORGE BARAGONA

George Baragona was a star athlete in Slidell in the late 1930s. When WWII started, he joined the Army and was assigned to the 507th P.I.R. 82nd Airborne. During the invasion of Normandy, his company was dropped behind enemy lines, but unfortunately dropped several miles off target in a swamp.

They made their way through the swamp to the village of Graignes, France, where they were welcomed and fed by the villagers. They fortified the village using a 12th century church as a fort. When the Germans came, they successfully defended the village for two days, but on the third day the Germans were successful. Pvt. George Baragona and several of his comrades were marched from the church, made to dig their own grave, and executed. The Germans then rounded up many of the villagers who had aided them, both men and women, and executed them in the same fashion. After the war no one was held accountable for this atrocity.

Private Baragona's remains were repatriated and rest today in Our Lady of Lourdes Cemetery in Slidell.

—BY JOHN CASE

Did you know?

Did you know that in the 1930s and 40s, the newspaper would print that Errol Flynn, Greta Garbo, Humphrey Bogart or some other great actor or actress was in town? This simply meant a movie starring them was playing at the Arcade.

Did you know that Ricky Nelson and James Brown performed here?

EDITOR'S NOTE: John Case has written a number of short pieces on individuals who have lived in Slidell that we sprinkled throughout this book identified as *SNIPPETS FROM THE PAST* and *DID YOU KNOW?* Case is a native of Mississippi who moved to Slidell in 1973. He has for many years written fiction for fun with most of his stories being based on growing up in rural Mississippi. Recently, he has been writing fact-based stories that feature Slidell and St. Tammany Parish. Case has had articles published in newspapers and magazines and is married to long-time Slidell native Brenda Lowry. They have two sons, Christopher and Alan. He uses the name J.S. Case in most of his writing so as not to be confused with the famous novelist John Case.

Politics As Unusual

Lawrence "Floppy" Abney is being pedaled down Carey Street by Ed Randal after winning a political bet. According to Ann Cappel, Floppy's daughter, her dad never lost a bet to Ed.

<small>Photo courtesy of Ann Cappel.</small>

The "Sleepy" Village

Many residents who have come to Slidell in the last 20 years or so may find it difficult to imagine what a "sleepy little village" Slidell was in the 40s and 50s, according to newspaper reporter Larry Ciko, who grew up during that time.

"There were no hospitals, supermarkets or shopping centers. Roads were gravel (which wasn't a problem because there wasn't much traffic). There was one traffic light at Front and Fremaux because it was the intersection of U.S. 11 and U.S. 190."

Slidell High stood where Slidell Junior High is now located. Our Lady of Lourdes School and convent were on Second Street in buildings now housing City Hall. The Arcade Theater, also in Olde Towne, Ciko remembers, charged 15 cents admission and five cents each for a bag of popcorn and a Coke. Names of Slidell's first families come to mind as he talks about Abney's Western Auto Store, Haas' five and dime, McDaniel's clothing store, Neuhauser's Department Store, Garrett's car dealership, Johnson's Cleaners, Sarraille's food store, Giordano-Buckley Shoes, and Cusimano's Drug Store, to name a few.

"Homer G. Fritchie was the only mayor I knew when I was growing up. He took office 11 years before I was born and left office when I was 21!"

Although those businesses have closed and the buildings have been updated or razed, their owners' roots are deeply planted in the Slidell of today.

Ciko remembers Bosco's Restaurant on Pontchartrain Drive, a Slidell landmark for several generations. Its owner, "Mr. Sam" Bosco was more than a restaurateur; he was a remarkable man who left an indelible mark on the city.

When he moved to Slidell in 1943, he bought a building that was half inside and half outside of the city limits. "We had to make sure the slot machines and fireworks were on the side of the room that was outside of the city limits," Bosco stated in an interview. As the business thrived, he added a motel and expanded the restaurant and lounge.

Noted musicians playing in the nightclub were "Fats" Domino, Papa Celestin and Tony Almerico, who had a live radio broadcast on Sundays in the 1940s.

Bosco's served as a meeting, eating, and partying place for residents and travelers. The restaurant's policy was not to deny food to anyone who could not pay. His generosity also extended to the city he loved. He helped fund the building of the bleachers at the former site of Slidell High School and aided in the purchase of band uniforms. Much of his charitable work was done anonymously, only disclosed at his death in 1981 by those who were the recipients of his generosity. An example of his generosity was his donation of funds toward the construction of the bell tower at Old Lady of Lourdes Church.

Mr. Bosco was also the owner of Domino Farm at Alton and was one of the pioneer thoroughbred horse breeders in St. Tammany Parish.

THE BAR AT ST. CHRISTOPHER'S CURVE INN WAS A POPULAR GATHERING SPOT IN THE 50S. PHOTO COURTESY OF LYDIA NELSON

EARLY SCHOOLS

Private schools existed in Slidell as early as 1890. The first substantial public school located at the present site of Brock Elementary, erected in 1910, included grades 1-11. This school was restricted to white children. A black public school was erected about the same time, named St. Tammany, and built across the street from today's St. Tammany Jr. High.

Slidell High School was completed in 1924 on Third St. between Maine and Pennsylvania. This is now the site of Slidell Junior High. Slidell High was the first accredited high school in St. Tammany parish.

SLIDELL HIGH SCHOOL

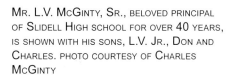

MR. L.V. McGINTY, SR., BELOVED PRINCIPAL OF SLIDELL HIGH SCHOOL FOR OVER 40 YEARS, IS SHOWN WITH HIS SONS, L.V. JR., DON AND CHARLES. PHOTO COURTESY OF CHARLES McGINTY

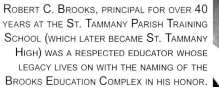

ROBERT C. BROOKS, PRINCIPAL FOR OVER 40 YEARS AT THE ST. TAMMANY PARISH TRAINING SCHOOL (WHICH LATER BECAME ST. TAMMANY HIGH) WAS A RESPECTED EDUCATOR WHOSE LEGACY LIVES ON WITH THE NAMING OF THE BROOKS EDUCATION COMPLEX IN HIS HONOR.

PHOTOS OF MR. BROOKS, ST. TAMMANY HIGH AND SLIDELL HIGH SCHOOL COURTESY ST. TAMMANY PARISH SCHOOL BOARD

Historic Landmarks

A walk through Greenwood Cemetery is a walk through history. You'll find the names of Slidell's "first citizens" resting in eternal peace among beautiful oaks and stately pines.

Once a Roman Catholic church of white parishioners, this beautiful wooden building is now home to Mt. Olive AME Church with an African American congregation—both worshipping the same God.

Pen & Ink Drawings
by Wanda Reiss Jenson

Dee's Funeral Beans

1	tablespoon vegetable oil
1	large onion, chopped
1	pound ground beef
1	tablespoon vinegar
1/3	cup ketchup
3/4	cup brown sugar, packed
1	(15.5-ounce) can pork and beans, undrained
1	(15.5-ounce) can lima beans, undrained
1	(15.5-ounce) can kidney beans, undrained
	Salt and black pepper to taste

Preheat oven to 350 degrees.

Heat oil in a large skillet and brown onion and ground beef, breaking beef apart with a fork as it cooks. Drain oil and return meat to pan.

Stir in all remaining ingredients and mix very well. Bake about 1 hour before serving.

Did you know?

Did you know that there are rows of graves marked with simple crosses along the ditch in Greenwood Cemetery? This is the resting place of the poor, or the unknowns, the John and Jane Does. This is our Potters Field. What interesting stories may lie in secret with the unknowns!

—by John Case

Living The American Dream

What do you get when a smiling New Orleans Irish potato famine girl meets a serious Mississippi Delta boy? You get a perfect combination of love and laughter that endured for 49 years.

Chuck and Myra Blackwell were ordinary people living in extraordinary times. They had experienced economic depression and world wars, and were raising a family during the tumultuous 60's. But amidst all of that unrest they created a peaceful, happy existence for their family, and helped establish the wonderful city of Slidell we all love.

In 1958, with three daughters and their young son in tow, the Blackwells made the trek across Lake Pontchartrain. They settled in the sleepy little town of Slidell in pursuit of "the American Dream". Soon thereafter, they opened the Slidell Credit

CHARLES AND MYRA BLACKWELL
COURTESY OF KATHRYN B. JONES

Bureau on Cousin Street (in what is now "Old Towne") between Georg's Hotel and Haas 5 & 10. At that time, Slidell was on the verge of a population explosion, With the advent of the space program and creation of the NASA Michoud site in New Orleans and Stennis Space Center in nearby Mississippi, the city's population nearly tripled. The influx of new residents, coupled with Chuck and Myra's hard work and the support of dedicated employees, resulted in the Credit Bureau's success. For thirty years the Blackwells provided jobs and forged relationships with hundreds of Slidell residents, both young and old.

Vanilla Wafer Cake

- 2 sticks margarine, softened (not butter)
- 2 cups granulated sugar
- 6 eggs
- 1 (12-ounce) box vanilla wafers, finely crushed
- 1/2 cup milk
- 1 cup chopped pecans
- 1 (7-ounce) bag flaked coconut

Preheat oven to 300 degrees. Grease and flour a 12-cup Bundt pan and set aside.

In a mixing bowl, thoroughly combine margarine and sugar. Add eggs one at a time, beating well after each addition. Add wafer crumbs alternately with milk, mixing well. Stir in pecans and coconut, blending to incorporate into batter.

Pour mixture into prepared pan and bake for about 90 minutes. Remove cake from oven and allow to rest on a rack for about 10 minutes before removing it from the pan. Invert cake on a serving plate.

Note: According to this contributor, removing the cake from the pan immediately out of the oven will result in your having a large cookie rather than a cake! The cake is super moist and the recipe converts to cupcakes with an adjustment for cooking time.

Jan Brown worked for the Blackwells for twenty years and remained friends, knowing Myra fifty years! "My fondest memories are of the times shared at Christmas Open Houses, Credit Women functions, and gatherings at their home for staff and their families. Throughout their lives, they fostered relationships in a community that shared the same values of honesty, responsibility, patriotism and respect. Through their business and in their private lives, they devoted their time and talents to faithfully serving others. Their common sense and optimism embodied everything they did."

As a couple, Chuck and Myra were inseparable; they worked together, they gardened together, they travelled together. When the love of her life died in 1995, Myra was heartbroken. But like all strong Southern women, she forged on with dignity and strength, beginning a new life, yet celebrating the life she and Chuck had created. She became active in numerous organizations, most notably the Slidell Garden Club, where she nurtured the hobby that she and Chuck loved the most. On February 24, 2011, Myra Blackwell passed away peacefully at her home in Brugier. It's a blessing to know that she and Chuck are together once more.

In many ways, Chuck and Myra were typical of their generation, but in other ways, so distinctively unique. Their legacy has given us many life's lessons that we will cherish for our families and in our Slidell community for generations to come.

Snippet from the Past

ARTHUR CHEVROLET

Arthur Chevrolet was one of three brothers that built the first Chevrolet automobile. Financial problems forced them to sell the company and it was absorbed by General Motors. They then began racing cars and building race cars. Arthur raced in the first Indianapolis 500.

His brother Gaston was killed in an automobile race, and Arthur and his brother Louis built a newly designed airplane engine. It was called the Chevrolair. Again financial problems plagued the company and it was taken over by Martin Aircraft Company. Martin Aircraft became Martin Marietta and eventually Lockheed Martin.

For some unknown reason Arthur moved to Slidell and in 1946 hanged himself at a house on Carey Street. He died a pauper and is buried in an unmarked grave in Indianapolis next to his brothers, Gaston and Louis.

--- BY JOHN CASE

Fig Cake

Cake:
2   cups all-purpose flour
1 1/2 cups granulated sugar
1   teaspoon salt
1   teaspoon baking soda
1   teaspoon nutmeg
1   teaspoon cloves
1   teaspoon cinnamon
1   cup vegetable oil
3   eggs, lightly beaten
1   cup buttermilk
1   teaspoon vanilla
1   cup fig preserves
1   cup chopped pecans

Preheat oven to 325 degrees; spray a Bundt pan with cooking spray and set aside.

Sift together all dry ingredients. Add oil, eggs, buttermilk and vanilla.

Mix well and add fig preserves and pecans. Stir to incorporate and pour mixture into prepared pan. Bake for one hour and pour on Glaze immediately.

Glaze:
1   stick butter, melted
1   cup buttermilk
1/2   tablespoon light corn syrup
1   teaspoon baking soda
1/2   teaspoon vanilla

Mix all ingredients except vanilla and cook 10 minutes, stirring constantly. Remove from heat and stir in vanilla.

Spoon Glaze over hot cake as soon as it comes from the oven.

FOOTPRINTS ON OUR HEARTS...

Slidell's history is filled with farmers and engineers, teachers and artists, business people, full-time homemakers and volunteers. Some are known to many and others known only to a few.

Some places that delighted people for years no longer exist. Businesses that were successful have vanished. Some were victims of "progress," others just outlived their purpose. The charm of Olde Town's specialty stores could not survive the retail fever of new shopping malls. However, Olde Town flourishes today with antique and decorating shops, entertainment spots, and restaurants. Quaint cottages now house attorney offices, beauty salons and coffee shops.

Each person who has lived, or is living, in Slidell contributed and continues to contribute to its unique inheritance and future. Some stayed only a short while, others until their deaths, each leaving marks of their gifts and talents.

This book is a tribute to all who left footprints on the soil and on our hearts.

JOSEPH DOUCETTE
PHOTO COURTESY OF
ALICE D. TWILLIE

PETE AND LUCY PRAVATA
PHOTO BY GILDA PERKINS
COURTESY OF ARRIOLLIA "BONNY" VANNEY

Coconut Pound Cake

2 sticks butter
4 tablespoons margarine
3 cups granulated sugar
6 eggs
1 teaspoon vanilla
3 cups unsifted all-purpose flour
1 cup milk
2 (3.5-ounce) cans flaked coconut

Preheat oven to 300 degrees. Grease a 10-inch tube pan and set aside.

In a large mixing bowl with an electric mixer, cream butter, margarine and sugar until well blended. Add eggs, one at a time, and beat until mixture is light and fluffy. Add vanilla. At low speed, alternately add flour (3/4 cup at a time) with milk (1/3 cup at a time); beginning and ending with the flour. Add coconut and beat until well blended.

Spoon mixture into prepared pan and bake for 2 hours or until tester comes out clean. Cool cake in the pan on a rack for at least 15 minutes before inverting it on a plate.

Long Macaroni and Cheese

1 (12-ounce) package long macaroni
2 teaspoons salt
6 tablespoons butter or margarine, divided
2 eggs, lightly beaten
1 1/2 cups evaporated milk
Salt and black pepper to taste
1 (16-ounce) block extra sharp Cheddar cheese, cubed or grated
1/2 cup dry breadcrumbs

Fill a large pot with 3 quarts of water and bring to a boil; add macaroni and salt and cook, uncovered, for about 7 minutes. Drain pasta and return to pot.

Preheat oven to 375 degrees. Spray a baking dish with cooking spray and set aside.

Add 4 tablespoons butter to pasta and stir well. In a separate bowl, combine eggs and evaporated milk; stir into pasta and add seasonings to taste. Spoon half of macaroni mixture into prepared dish and top with half the cheese. Add remaining macaroni and cover top with remaining cheese.

Sprinkle with breadcrumbs and dot with remaining 2 tablespoons of butter. Bake until bubbling and golden browned, about 30-40 minutes.

Kumquat Marmalade

50 kumquats
1 orange
2 lemons
Sugar
Certo pectin

Slice kumquats, orange and lemons very thinly; removing seeds. Measure fruit as it is added to a stock pot or other large container. Add water to cover fruit and set aside overnight, or 12-15 hours.

Boil fruit in water for 15 minutes. For each cup of fruit measured after slicing, add 1 cup of sugar to the mixture. Bring to a rolling boil and add pectin (determine amount according to package directions). Boil for 5 minutes.

Allow mixture to rest for a short time to prevent fruit from coming to the top. Ladle marmalade into hot sterile glass jars and seal with lids and rings.

Note: Prepare jars by placing them in a baking dish and pouring about an inch of hot water into the pan. This will make 8 or 9 half-pint jars.

These are treasured recipes from Garden Club members who are gone but not forgotten... Ann Flotte and Colinda Massamini.

SLIDELL, THE CAMELLIA CITY

Just as the railroad brought the first industry and more people to Slidell, the 1960s brought the space program and an influx of families from across the nation. Slidell soon blossomed into the metropolitan city that it is today.

The talents, gifts, energy and ideas these people brought with them created a city with the best schools in the state, National Merit Scholars and star athletes. The arts and cultural opportunities of our city soon surpassed those in much larger cities.

The civic pride of our community is evident

in the many service organizations, garden clubs, social clubs for men, women and children, and several Mardi Gras Krewes.

In 1986, when Lionel Washington was President of the City Council, Councilmen Bob Callahan and Phil Salvaggio presented a proclamation naming Slidell "The Camellia City" which was passed by the Council.

As you begin to savor our city through these next few pages, you'll realize the generosity, the love and the relationships we share and cherish.

MAYOR FREDDY DRENNAN

OIL ON CANVAS BY RICHARD A. RAY

Dear Citizens,

It is my pleasure to serve you and this great city. I've been fortunate to travel and represent Slidell many times. Over the course of traveling, people always ask you where you're from. Here's what I tell them.

I live in a city that has the best schools in the state. We have a very low crime rate, thanks to our great police department. Slidell has 32 parks, and it's not unusual to see children playing and ladies jogging early in the morning or late at night.

We live in a city that provides all the amenities of a great metropolitan area, with the shopping, entertainment and benefits that a big city provides. Slidell has some of the best food in the world and cultural activities thrive here. You want it, we have it.

Louisiana is a sportsman's paradise, and Slidell is no exception: from the murky waters of its bayous to one of the largest salt water lakes in the world providing easy access to the Gulf of Mexico. What more could you ask for?

I am proud to call Slidell my home. It truly is the best kept secret in the south.

Your mayor,

NASA

When the NASA Michoud Computer Operations Office was opened in Slidell in 1962, it was one of the largest high-speed electronic computer centers in the United States.

With the computer office in Slidell, the Stennis Testing center 20 miles to the north, and the Michoud Assembly Center 20 miles to the south, Slidell was at the center of the space age. In five years, the population of Slidell grew from 6,000 to 16,000 and Slidell became the largest city in St. Tammany Parish.

Homemade Irish Cream

1 3/4 cups liquor of choice (Irish whiskey, brandy, rum, Scotch or rye whiskey)
1 (14-ounce) can sweetened condensed milk
1 cup heavy cream
4 eggs
2 tablespoons chocolate-flavored syrup
2 teaspoons instant coffee granules
1 teaspoon vanilla
1/2 teaspoon almond extract

In the jar of a blender, combine all ingredients and blend until smooth and well mixed.

Serve over ice, or as desired.

This mixture will keep for up to 1 month in the refrigerator. Simply pour it into a clean glass container with a screw-top. Stir well before using.

Keep in mind that raw eggs are a health issue for some. You may substitute an equal amount of a pasteurized egg product with no discernable change to the outcome.

NASA's computer center at Slidell supported the New Orleans assembly plant and more.

ON SEPTEMBER 30TH, 2010, AFTER 37 YEARS AND 136 TANKS DELIVERED, LOCKHEED MARTIN PRODUCTION OF THE SPACE SHUTTLE EXTERNAL TANK CAME TO AN END AT THE NASA MICHOUD ASSEMBLY FACILITY AT THE NORTH EASTERN EDGE OF NEW ORLEANS, DIRECTLY ACROSS PONTCHARTRAIN FROM SLIDELL.
—PHOTO COURTESY OF LOCKEED MARTIN

Easy Breezy Summer Punch

1   (89-ounce) container orange juice, chilled
1   (46-ounce) can pineapple juice, chilled
1   (2-litre) bottle ginger ale, chilled

In a large container, mix all ingredients. Serve over ice.

This makes about 25 1-cup servings and is easy and great for a large group.

Easy Fruit Cobbler

8   tablespoons butter or margarine
1   cup self-rising flour
1   cup granulated sugar
2   cup milk
     cups blueberries or sliced peaches

Preheat oven to 350 degrees.

Place butter in an 8 x 10-inch baking dish and set in oven to melt while other ingredients are prepared.

Mix together flour, sugar and milk and stir until lumps are gone. Pour dough batter over the melted butter and spoon fruit over the top. Do not stir!

Bake for 35 to 40 minutes.

THYME
MIXED MEDIA HALEY CUTRER
TEEN ARTIST OF THE YEAR 2010

THE REINE FAMILY

ROOTED IN ST. TAMMANY PARISH

George Ernest Reine, Jr., entered the world on June 13, 1919, and began his journey down the road to establishing the family name as one of the premier construction companies in the Slidell area. He joined the U.S. Army Air Corp in 1941, serving four years at an air base in India. During his service he corresponded with his sweetheart, Bertha Miller. Within two weeks of his return to the states, he and Bertha were married. When George and Bertha moved their family from Mandeville to Slidell in 1950, he began building and developing in Slidell, which was experiencing a period of economic and industrial growth.

He founded Reine Construction, which was at the forefront of the residential boom that would provide housing for the new residents. The company quickly earned a reputation for quality construction and well-designed custom residential properties. He branched into other business ventures which included Ozone Realty, Builders Center of Slidell and H.A. Davis Lumber Company. His building of numerous residential communities, schools and prominent structures in the community enhanced the Camellia City's prosperity. In addition to their businesses, both George and Bertha were involved in civic and charitable work.

GEORGE AND BERTHA REINE

They had five sons: George III, Ronald, Glen, Michael and Timothy. All five continued in the industry for another generation, focusing on further enhancing the appeal of Slidell, the city they all called "home." George and Bertha's legacy of philanthropy, including land donations for schools and recreational areas, charitable donations to the church and the Slidell Women's Civic Club, and their participation in city development, continued with their children and grandchildren.

Along with his brothers, Ronald Reine inherited the same passion for land development and building construction that had identified his father. In 1980, Ronald met Sylvia Tannehill on a blind date arranged by a mutual friend. "It was love at first sight," admits Sylvia. They were married on Jan. 30, 1981. Their dear friend, Becky Kennedy, who was responsible for their meeting, constantly reminds them that "she does good work."

Together, the couple founded Omni Construction, Inc., originally specializing in developing quality residential communities throughout the South and the U.S. Virgin Islands. The company later expanded into providing disaster recovery services across the United States and to islands in the Caribbean. Ronald and Sylvia's four children, Deanna, Laura, Brian, and Jason, have each been involved with the company and have developed expertise in disaster removal and recovery. Omni

RONNIE AND SYLVIA REINE

Construction became Omni Pinnacle LLC, run by Ronald and his son, Brian.

Their expertise proved invaluable at 9:45 a.m. on August 29, 2005, when the western eye wall of Hurricane Katrina, at Category

—continued

THE REINE FAMILY

Three, passed through St. Tammany Parish. The resulting storm surge impacted all 57 miles of coastline of the parish and extended more than six miles inland. Slidell was inundated with a surge of 13 to 16 feet, as were many other communities in the parish. Katrina damaged 48,792 housing units in St. Tammany Parish alone, and Omni Pinnacle was among the first on the scene, providing emergency disaster services to the parish and the cities of New Orleans and Abita Springs. The company played a major role in the area-wide clean-up effort that collected more than 6.6 million cubic yards of debris. On behalf of a grateful City, New Orleans Mayor Ray Nagin presented Omni Pinnacle an award for outstanding contributions to the remembrance, renewal, and rebirth of New Orleans and the City of Slidell presented Ronald with a *Katrina Angel Award* for his donation of debris removal at Our Lady of Lourdes Church.

Omni remains in the vanguard of residential subdivision construction with many of the area's best known communities and commercial developments are a result of their work.

Also in the aftermath of Katrina, Sylvia and Ronald transformed what had been historic properties on Front Street, many damaged beyond repair, into La Reine Olde Towne Centre. The popular commercial center now includes a number of retail shops, stores, and services as well as offices for the family's businesses.

La Reine Olde Towne Centre is home to Three Divas and Sugardaddy Fine Gifts. Ronald, the "Sugardaddy" in the equation, had approached Sylvia with the idea of opening a gift shop in the Centre. Sylvia immediately thought of her daughter, Laura, and daughter-in-law, Leonette Loe, as the two women who should join her in becoming the "Three Divas." Together, they established the trendy store as a source for gifts in any price range, as well as men's and women's clothing and accessories.

AN APPRECIATIVE COMMUNITY

Success is measured in numerous ways, but probably none as meaningful as the grateful appreciation of neighbors for the contributions made to the improvement of the quality of life in the community where you live. Using this barometer to measure their accomplishments, the Reine family has written an important chapter in the history and growth of Slidell and St. Tammany Parish. One inspiration for preserving the family's history for future generations is Ronald's aunt, Lucy Miller Band.

Driven by their belief that "community involvement is inborn," Ronald's family donated a portion of land in the Tuscany subdivision to

OLD WHITE KITCHEN

be utilized as a park. In addition, the family gifted a Rosary Garden to St. Luke's Catholic Church and contributed to the Society of St. Teresa of Jesus.

Feeling that the needs of children should be uppermost in their efforts to shape a bright future for the parish, the Reine family has long supported Children's Hospital and other organizations that focus on the needs of young people. A grateful Children's Hospital noted Omni Pinnacle's generosity in helping to raise $1.3 million in support of the 2008 Children's Hospital telethon. The Hospital also recognized the company's invaluable participation in making their Annual Allfax Specialties Golf Classic, hosted by Deuce McAllister in 2007, the most successful in the event's history. The Dream Factory of Louisiana, which works to fulfill the dreams of critically and chronically ill chil-

dren in the Tri-Parish area, sent their appreciation for the company's support of their "Buzz the Red, White, and Blue, Make a Dream Come True" event in 2008.

Other recipients of the Reine family's philanthropic efforts include the Children's Wish Foundation, the Christopher Condon Cool Doctor Foundation, the Sunny Glen Children's Home, Our Lady of Lourdes Catholic Church, the United Christian Concern, and numerous other civic and charitable organizations.

In addition, the family's efforts in providing disaster services to communities throughout the Southeast, the Atlantic Coast, and abroad, have garnered praise and awards from local, state, and foreign governments as well as agencies and departments of the U.S. government. Omni has worked closely with the U.S. Army Corps of Engineers, the

—continued

LA REINE OLDE TOWN CENTRE

THE REINE FAMILY

National Park Service, and the U.S. Navy on numerous disaster relief efforts.

In 2007, Omni Pinnacle was singled out by its peers in the industry with the "Large Contractor of the Year" award. Four years later, the East St. Tammany Chamber of Commerce presented the Reine family with the prestigious honor of receiving the first "Economic Development Pioneer Award" for the family's support since the Chamber was founded in 1962. The entire Reine family was in attendance at the awards ceremony where they were honored as having been instrumental in the construction of Slidell, beginning with development of some of the first neighborhoods. The family has owned construction companies, retail outlets and supply stores, and, continues to develop Slidell. With the rebuilding of the White Kitchen in Slidell and the first branded hotel in Pearl River, the Reine family continues to foster economic development in our region with seven active Chamber businesses.

Ronald Reine points out his own meter for gauging the success he and his family have enjoyed in St. Tammany Parish: "One of my greatest rewards, has been being able to work with my wife, Sylvia, Omni's Vice-President, and to share our accomplishments together. I feel that being a happy, contented man with a loving wife, children, and grandchildren, whom I love, is a success in itself."

THE ENTIRE REINE FAMILY WAS IN ATTENDANCE AT THE AWARDS CEREMONY WHERE THEY WERE HONORED AS HAVING BEEN INSTRUMENTAL IN THE CONSTRUCTION OF SLIDELL, BEGINNING WITH DEVELOPMENT OF SOME OF THE FIRST NEIGHBORHOODS.

Langiappe

Garden Tip:

For propagating finicky shrubs, cut a slip of your plant on the diagonal. Put the cutting immediately into a hole in a small potato. Prepare the ground or a container for planting, add compost if available, set the potato into soil, and cover it completely, leaving only the cutting above the surface. Water gently and keep moist. It's almost foolproof for starting stubborn, woody plants.

"Prepare the soil and you will delight in lush reward."

This hint is from the Lakewood Garden Club, founded in 1971 with Mrs. Alvin Cuserta and Mrs. Rubin Wooten as founding members.

THREE GREEN LEAVES
STONEWARE CLAY BY ANN STUART

Party Cheesecakes

24 vanilla wafers
2 (8-ounce) packages cream cheese, softened
3/4 cup sugar
2 eggs, lightly beaten
1 tablespoon lemon juice
1 teaspoon vanilla
1 (22-ounce) can cherry pie filling
Sweetened whipped cream, optional

Preheat oven to 350 degrees. Place a paper liner in each of 24 mini muffin cups, then place a vanilla wafer in each of them.

Combine cream cheese, sugar, eggs, lemon juice and vanilla. Beat at medium speed until well blended and smooth. Spoon enough filling into each cup to fill about 2/3 full. Bake for about 15 to 20 minutes.

Cool thoroughly or refrigerate overnight. Immediately before serving, spoon cherry pie filling on each cheesecake. Top with a dollop of sweetened whipped cream, if desired.

Monkey Bread

1 cup granulated sugar
2 tablespoons ground cinnamon
4 (10-count) cans buttermilk biscuits
8 tablespoons melted butter

Preheat oven to 350 degrees.

In a large mixing bowl, combine sugar and cinnamon. Separate biscuits and cut into quarters, dropping them into the mixing bowl. Cover the bowl well and shake until all biscuit pieces are well coated.

Place coated biscuits into a Bundt pan and pour the melted butter evenly over the pieces.

Bake for 30 minutes or until golden browned and puffy.

Dynamic Duo

Reverend and Mrs. John Ellermann

For 58 years, John and Elva Ellermann have worked side-by-side as husband and wife, faithfully serving the members of their church and the community at large.

The couple first arrived in Slidell in 1970. John was the newly elected president of the Southern District of the Lutheran Church-Missouri Synod whose job it was to oversee all of the congregations in

Reverend and Mrs. John Ellermann

Louisiana, Mississippi, Alabama, and the Florida panhandle. Elva's job was to run the house and raise four children (on a pastor's salary!) Together they helped plant and grow the Lutheran church in the South at a time when "What's a Lutheran?" was a common query.

As a gifted preacher and teacher, John drew members through his novel approach to the Gospel message, the "Pipeline." On Sundays, his captivating children's sermons, based on that week's scripture message, contained object lessons (and an occasional ostrich egg, live critter – even a snake once!) entertaining and educating young and old alike. John visited members in their homes, at the hospital, and in nursing homes, fostering personal relationships that helped create a strong sense of community.

Elva shared her talents by directing the choir, leading JOY Bible Study, and managing the quilters. In 2009, she received the "LANO," the Louisiana Non-Profit Organization Heroine Award, for her dedication to this worthy cause. Together their strong leadership and extraordinary work ethic helped grow church membership exponentially and establish a solid Lutheran presence in Slidell.

Amazingly, both made time to pursue a mutual hobby---wood crafting. John and Elva fashioned a variety of craft items (ornaments, rocking horses, Santas) which they sometimes sold, but more often gave as cherished gifts.

Parson's People

As their expertise grew, they created a world of unique little figures and named them "Parsons People." Since 1989, John has hand carved each figure out of basswood; Elva paints each one with painstaking detail. Every "person" is named, numbered and signed. These one-of-a-kind creations have earned John and Elva the official designation as Louisiana Craftsmen.

In 1992, the couple officially "retired." Since then they've served five more congregations, still teach Bible study, and continue to participate in many aspects of church life. John counsels, writes and presents papers. Elva quilts, sews, and participates in various local philanthropic organizations.

JOY Bible Study

Elva's Quilters

"For you make me glad by your deeds, O Lord; I sing for JOY at the works of your hands." Psalm 92:4

God's workmanship is evident in the wonderful people and beautiful places that are Slidell. For more than 30 years, one group of ladies has shared its time, talent, and treasures in a unique way.

Founded in 1974, a small group of Lutheran women began meeting monthly for Bible study and adopted the name JOY (Jesus, Others, You). The membership grew to include several talented ladies with a penchant for quilting. The quilters soon established their own monthly gatherings, creating lap robes for local nursing homes, crib and cot blankets, as well as large, colorful quilts which were shipped around the world through the non-profit Lutheran World Relief.

With both JOY Bible Study and the quilters desiring to put their faith into action, the two groups formed a collaborative effort and the annual JOY Spring Charity Auction was born. Prior to auction, the multi-talented JOY ladies make unique hand-crafted items, bake delicious treats, and grow native plants to sell. It became know as "make, bake, grow." The quilters work diligently throughout the year, designing and creating hundreds of finely crafted quilts to be sold to the highest bidders.

Since the first auction in 1980, proceeds of over $120,000 have been donated to local, national, and worldwide charities. In addition, well over 4500 quilts have been lovingly stitched to be sold at auction, donated to missions, and given to those in need.

PHOTO COURTESY OF GWYN ELLERMANN

Founding member Elva Ellermann speaks for the both organizations when she says, "It's a lot of hard work, but we truly get back as much as we give. We're honored to have the opportunity to enrich our community."

NORTHLAKE ORAL AND MAXILLOFACIAL SURGERY

Dr. Russ Westfall has been practicing oral surgery in Slidell and Mandeville since completing his residency in 1979 at Charity Hospital – LSU Medical Center in New Orleans. A Diplomat of the American Board of Oral & Maxillofacial Surgery and a Fellow of the American Association of Oral & Maxillofacial Surgeons, Dr. Westfall has been recognized by his peers as one of the Northshore's most respected dentists.

Dr. Westfall is joined by his wife, Nancy, a registered nurse, and a staff of sixteen professionals in providing the highest quality oral and maxillofacial surgical services to patients in St. Tammany Parish.

"Nancy and I and our entire staff are committed to providing our patients with the most courteous and prompt state-of-the-art oral and maxillofacial surgical care which incorporates the most up-to-date technology and scientific information available today," Dr. Westfall states. "We are also committed to giving back to the Northshore community by actively supporting our church, the Chamber of Commerce, the Slidell Department of Cultural Affairs, and the Slidell Symphony Society whose mission is to provide educational and cultural musical enrichment for students and adults in the greater Slidell area.

PHOTOS OF SLIDELL SYMPHONY SOCIETY'S SALON CONCERTS COURTESY OF KAY TAYLOR

Appreciation of the arts is an integral part of the city of Slidell. Began as the "The Slidell Performing Arts Guild" in the 1950s, and later incorporated as The Slidell Symphony Society, it has provided educational and musical enrichment for the people of greater Slidell. Concerts for children are performed in area schools; "The Nutcracker" is performed yearly, as well as concerts in the park. Pictured at left is the setting of a "Salon Concert," given at member's homes, with a wonderful meal followed by a performance. Dr. Russ and Nancy Westfall have been instrumental in developing this splendid program.

Le Cotillion

Le Cotillion is a social organization that was formed in 1972 with 46 charter members. Its main purpose is to formally present young ladies to the community as debutantes.

The official season begins in June of each year with an introduction luncheon followed by parties, teas and multiple activities for the debutantes and their escorts. The season culminates with a formal presentation ball held in January.

SLIDELL LITTLE THEATRE

Slidell Little Theatre, the premier community theatre in St. Tammany Parish, was founded in 1963 by volunteers who recognized the need for live theatre on the Northshore. Early productions were staged in high school auditoriums before finally graduating to today's state-of-the-art facility located at 2024 Nellie Drive.

Each year this all volunteer, not-for-profit organization entertains approximately 10,000 adults and children with high quality theatrical productions. SLT devotes the entire summer to educating school age children through its Young Actors Theatre of Slidell program (YATS), designed to introduce young people from preschool to high school seniors to the stage, ensuring an enduring stable of patrons and actors for the Theatre's next 50 years.

RAGTIME STAGED APRIL – MAY 2010
COURTESY OF SLIDELL LITTLE THEATRE

Tropical Island Rum Cake

For cake:
1   cup chopped pecans or walnuts
1   (18-ounce) yellow cake mix (no pudding included)
1   (3.25-ounce) package vanilla instant pudding mix
4   eggs
1/2 cup cold water
1/2 cup vegetable oil
1/2 cup dark rum (80 proof)

Preheat oven to 325 degrees. Grease and flour a 10-inch tube or 12-cup Bundt pan. Sprinkle chopped nuts into bottom of the pan.

Mix all remaining cake ingredients and pour over nuts. Bake for 1 hour. Cool on a rack and remove from pan. Prick holes in top of cake with a skewer or fork. Drizzle glaze (below) over cooled cake.

For glaze:
8   tablespoons butter
1/4 cup water
1   cup granulated sugar
1/2 cup dark rum

Melt butter in a medium saucepan. Stir in water and sugar. Boil for 5 minutes, stirring constantly. Remove from heat and stir in rum before drizzling glaze over top and sides of cake.

Best Milk Punch Ever

1/2 cup sugar
1   gallon whole milk, divided
1/2 gallon premium vanilla ice cream
1   fifth good quality bourbon
4   ounces pure vanilla extract

Add sugar and about a cup of milk to a small saucepan. Heat over medium heat until sugar is just dissolved. Stir often to prevent overheating and scorching.

Cool slightly and add to remaining milk in a large mixing bowl.

Add ice cream to milk, break it up with a large spoon. Allow ice cream to melt completely and stir bourbon and vanilla extract. Serve immediately.

The punch mixture may be stored in the refrigerator for as long as a week or in the freezer much longer.

Ozone Camellia Club

Social Heart of the "Camellia City"

To fully appreciate the work done by the Ozone Camellia Club, one should know that back in the 1940s, a single camellia plant cost about $70 (in 1940 money!). It's then understandable that enjoyment of the beautiful camellias was available only to the affluent.

Thanks to the Ozone Camellia Club and the international horticulture society, the plants are now available to all who choose to join the ranks of camellia lovers!

Just as camellia plants grow and blossom, so has the Ozone Camellia Club. It is known for its membership that began as a small horticultural society and grew into today's organization of about 280 members. The focus of the group is horticultural as well as social.

Shortly after its founding in 1951, the Club began adding a series of social functions, cotillion balls, and Mardi Gras events that made it the epicenter of the social scene in Slidell and St. Tammany Parish. In addition to its much anticipated three-day festival each December, which includes a series of parties and special social events, the Club holds an annual banquet at Slidell's City Auditorium.

"This was the only social club in the area when I moved to Slidell in 1967," states Bob Stroud, who, along with his wife, Erin, joined the Ozone Camellia Club.

"The Club holds meetings on a monthly basis between May and September and sponsors a variety of social events throughout the year. We're proud to be an organization that brings couples together

by offering activities that appeal to husbands, as well as wives, and has thus become an integral part of the social scene in Slidell."

THE HUMAN TOUCH

'Tis the human touch in this world that counts,
The touch of your hand and mine,
Which means far more to the fainting heart
Than shelter and bread and wine:
For shelter is gone when the night is o're,
And bread lasts only a day,
But the touch of the hand and the sound of the voice
Sing on in the soul alway.

SPENCER MICHAEL FREE

Slidell prides itself on the many ways its citizens serve each other. Through individual efforts and the work of many organizations, Slidell cares for those in need. The Mt.Olive A.M.E. Feeding Ministry feeds the homeless, homebound and needy. Habitat for Humanity builds homes year round. The Battered Women's Shelter houses women and children who have suffered abuse. Community Christian Concern, a division of the Slidell Ministerial Alliance, helps to feed, clothe and provide essentials for any seeking their service. The Children's Wish Foundation grants wishes for terminally ill children and Toys for Tots gives gifts to children at Christmas.

STARC, organized in 1972, provides a life-time of ever changing services for infants, children and adults with developmental disabilities and their families. STARC Art, one of their programs, enables students to earn money while promoting growth, self- expression and pride.

WATERCOLOR BY MARY LOU GOVERNALE
COURTESY OF THE STARC ART PROGRAM

JUNIOR AUXILLIARY

The Slidell Junior Auxiliary's commitment to community can best be summed up in the opening words of the JA prayer:

"Send us, O God, as Thy messengers to the hearts without a home, to lives without love, to the crowds without a guide. Send us to the children whom none have blessed, to the famished whom none have visited, to the fallen whom none have lifted, to the bereaved whom none have comforted."

For more than 50 years, the women of Junior Auxiliary, through their thousands of hours of volunteer service, have enhanced the lives of all in the community.

LIONS CLUB

The Slidell Lions Club, founded in1928, is located in a home at 356 Cleveland Avenue, donated to the club in 1982 by the Canulette-Baker families. This club was instrumental in getting the first mail deliveries in Slidell. The city did not have house numbers or street signs and the postmaster required both before mail could be delivered. The Lions Club contracted with Angola Prison to have the signs made. The signs were placed by the city and mail deliveries soon began.

Many relate the Lions Club with their eye glass collection services, through which glasses are redistributed to those in need throughout the world. A little known fact is this project began in 1925 when Helen Keller addressed the Lions' International Convention in Ohio and charged them to be "Knights of the Blind."

The Slidell Lions co-host a barbecue event each year with the Slidell Rotary Club that draws cooks from around the nation and raises money for community services.

THE LIONS CLUB HOME AT
356 CLEVELAND AVENUE
PHOTO BY SHARON DeLONG

SLIDELL WOMEN'S CIVIC CLUB

The Slidell Women's Civic Club (SWCC) was formed in 1947 by Anita Breisacher, Blanche Carroll, Virginia Madison and Peggy Sollberger. Its purpose is to foster civic, cultural and social welfare of the community. The SWCC sponsored the first Mardi Gras Ball and Parade in Slidell to honor outstanding residents. Each year the club members, by secret ballot, select two residents to be honored as King and Queen Samaritan. Their identity is kept secret until they are presented to the community at a carnival ball in their honor. The maids and dukes making up the royal court are also selected for their contributions to the community.

Various fund raisers during the year as well as the proceeds from the ball, are used for community programs, and to assist needy families. Theclub remains very active, continuing its community service.

LADIES OF THE WOMEN'S CIVIC CLUB ENTERTAINING PATIENTS AT NORTH SHORE LIVING CENTER AT CHRISTMAS. FROM LEFT TO RIGHT—NELL LAPORTE, SHARON DELONG, VIOLA COCRAN, MARGIE CHERNIAK, ROSEMARY CLEMENT, BONNIE CLEMENT, MARTHA VAN DEVENTER, JOANN DEVER AND ELLEN LAMARQUE, KNEELING.

ROTARY CLUB

Rotary is an international service organization, founded in 1905, with 1.2 million members in over 34,000 clubs. The two Rotary clubs in Slidell have about 120 members.

The Rotary Club of Slidell Northshore donated a fourteen-foot pedestal clock to the City of Slidell to commemorate the club's 25th anniversary on March 27, 2009. The clock is part of the restoration of Olde Towne Slidell following the devastation of Hurricane Katrina. Initially situated in front of the old Slidell Municipal Auditorium , it was moved across the street when the building was torn down and now stands between the new Slidell City Council and Administrative Center and the renovated City Hall.

PHOTO OF CLOCK IN FRONT OF THE OLD CITY AUDITORIUM, COURTESY OF KEN THOMPSON.

HONORING OUR SERVICE HEROES

America, fair land of mine, home of the just and true,

All hail to thee, land of the free, and the Red-White-and Blue

BY ARTHUR NICHOLAS HOSKING

Slidellians have served and continue to serve their country. They served with pride in World Wars I and II as well as Korea, Vietnam and today in the war against terror. Their memory is kept alive through numerous veterans' organizations. ROTC is active in the high schools and many young Slidellians have been selected to attend West Point, Annapolis, and the Air Force Academy.

Memorial Park, maintained by the Slidell Garden Club, is the site of programs on Memorial Day and Veterans Day. Flags fly year round on city, private and business property. The Heritage Festival, held on July 4th is a chance for Slidellians to gather, picnic and watch a spectacular fireworks show - all for the love of the Red-White-and Blue.

Sugared Pecans

3 1/2 cups pecan halves
1/2   cup water
1   cup granulated sugar
1   teaspoon ground cinnamon
1/8   teaspoon allspice

Preheat oven to 400 degrees.

Spread pecan halves in a single layer on a baking sheet and bake about 8 minutes. Watch carefully to prevent their burning.

Meanwhile, in a heavy saucepan combine water, sugar and spices. Cook over medium heat to a soft ball stage (236 degrees).

Immediately drop the pecans into the syrup and stir gently with a wooden spoon to coat the pecans. Continue stirring until the syrup becomes sugary and starts to harden. Turn out on a cool surface and separate into pieces using 2 forks.

Cool completely and store in an airtight container.

MADELINE CARDWELL, DAUGHTER OF KELLI AND CHAD CARDWELL AND GRANDDAUGHTER OF SCOTTIE AND KEN KUHLMANN, RESTS AFTER ENJOYING THE HERITAGE FESTIVAL.

CELEBRATING FAMILIES

THE "HOPE OAK"

Like the branches of the mighty oak, Southern families' arms are wide, encompassing grandparents, cousins, aunts and uncles… some by birth…many by friendship. Family members are often neighbors; some neighbors become "family." Slidell families continue to grow with each wedding and birth. Like the roots of the mighty oak, the hearts of Slidellians remain rooted there regardless of where life takes them.

COUSINS FROM LEFT, JONATHAN HICKS, JAMES GALYON AND MATTHEW HICKS.
PHOTO BY TERRYL ALEXANDER HICKS

NEWLYWEDS STEWART AND JENNIFER JONES

KATHRYN AND MELISSA K. JONES WITH GRANDPARENTS CEQCIA AND IKE HALL
OAK PHOTO BY SHARON DELONG—COURTESY OF HOPE STEWART CROCKETT

CELEBRATING TRADITIONS

Traditional Southern charm in Slidell is evident in the many ways Slidellians socialize. They spend weeks planning neighborhood block parties, Old Town Art Evenings, an annual antique fair and Mardi Gras and St. Patrick's Day parades.

The July Fourth Heritage Festival, school fairs and concerts in the park keep Slidellians laughing, loving and enjoying life. Sport events, art classes, and dance lessons for young and old give everyone a chance to participate.

Beta Sigma Phi, a philanthropic sorority whose letters represent life, learning and friendship, has four chapters in Slidell. There are book clubs, Red Hat Organizations, and lunch bunches.

THE DREW BOUNDS FAMILY CELEBRATES HALLOWEEN WITH THEIR NEIGHBORS COMPLETE WITH A HAYRIDE AND A FESTIVE OUTDOOR MEAL. COURTESY OF TATUM BOUNDS

EACH YEAR THE FIRST UNITED METHODIST CHURCH PROVIDES AN ENORMOUS PUMPKIN PATCH FOR CHILDREN OF ALL AGES TO ENJOY.

Mardi Gras

Carnival, originally a religious event, begins on Twelfth Night (the twelfth night after Christmas, January 6, when the Three Kings arrived in Bethlehem), and ends on Mardi Gras (Fat Tuesday, the last day to celebrate before Ash Wednesday and the beginning of Lent).

Carnival season in Slidell is low keyed and family oriented. Slidell's first carnival ball was held by the Slidell Women's Civic Club in 1950 and their first parade was in 1961. The Krewe De La Boutte Dominique formed in 1965, followed by the Mystic Krewe of Perseus

FROM LEFT—KRISTEN DENISE HALL, JAMES HEYERDALE HALL, EUGENE R. ST. JEAN—KING PERSEUS XXXVIII, CAROLINE GRACE THIRSTRUP, LYNN WALKER-ST. JEAN—QUEEN ANDROMEDA XXXVIII, MARGARET MARY MORGAN, LAUREN NICOLE THIRSTRUP.

in 1970. Slidell's celebrations have grown to four Sunday afternoon parades, two night parades, a walking parade, two boat parades and the Krewe of Paws for four legged friends.

A Mardi Gras room has been added to the Slidell Museum. Under the direction of Bonnie Vanney, this room is filled with mementos and extensive scrapbooks, one for each crew. A visit to this room is a must for all carnival lovers as well as history buffs.

CHRISTMAS

TRUE COMMUNITY SPIRIT

Christmas, an important part of Slidell life, is celebrated with lights, wreaths and other festive decorations and activities.

"Christmas under the Stars" is a celebration in Griffith Park that involves the entire town. School children perform, carolers sing, organizations decorate trees, Santa arrives and people gather nightly to visit and celebrate the season.

The Slidell Junior Auxiliary organizes a tour of homes, beautifully decorated for the season. Many churches have musical programs open to the public. Organizations and churches make sure that every home has a festive meal and toys for all who need them. There is a true community spirit that fills the air.

PHOTO OF JOHN WOLFRAM, SON OF MIKE AND CAROL WOLFRAM; TAKEN AT THE HISTORIC SLIDELL TRAIN DEPOT DURING THE CITY'S ANNUAL "CHRISTMAS UNDER THE STARS" HOLIDAY VILLAGE TRAIN DISPLAY. THOUGH MUCH OF THE ORIGINAL DISPLAY WAS LOST TO HURRICANE KATRINA, VOLUNTEERS HAVE WORKED DILIGENTLY TO RESTORE WHAT REMAINS A MAGICAL HOLIDAY TRADITION.

THE WADLEIGH FAMILY CHRISTMAS CARD COURTESY OF KENDRA WADLEIGH.

This tip is from the Slidell Newcomer Garden Club, founded in 1962 under the direction of Barbara Nix. There are now 60 members who participate in helping the "Clean City Committee" and decorate a tree for "Christmas under the Stars."

"A garden is a peaceful spot where you can stop to reflect and catch a glimpse of life's deeper meaning," --- Lucille Crumley

FUTURE GARDENER
PHOTO OF EMMA KATHERINE IVY,
COURTESY OF CHARLOTTE ELIAS (GRANDMOTHER)

Artichoke Yummies

2 tablespoons olive oil
2 cloves garlic, pressed
2 (8.5 ounce) cans artichoke hearts, drained and mashed
2 eggs, lightly beaten
1/8 teaspoon ground red pepper
3/4 cup shredded Parmesan, divided
3/4 cup seasoned breadcrumbs, divided

In a medium skillet, heat olive oil over medium heat and sauté garlic for about 2 minutes. Still in artichokes, eggs and red pepper. Reduce heat to low and cook, stirring constantly, for about 5 minutes.

Remove from heat and stir in 1/2 cup of Parmesan and 1/2 cup breadcrumbs. Cool slightly and roll mixture into 1-inch balls. Combine remaining Parmesan and breadcrumbs in a shallow dish and roll balls lightly in mixture.

Chill until firm.

This recipe should make about 3 dozen appetizer servings...which will disappear quickly!

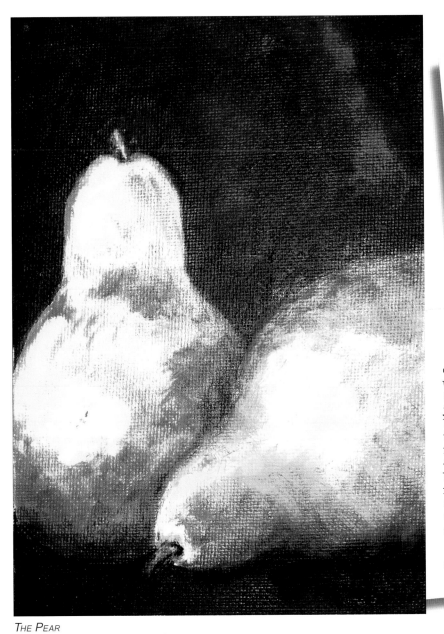

THE PEAR
OIL ON CANVAS—LYNDA DONALDSON

Cheesy Shrimp On Grits Toast

3   (14-ounce) cans chicken broth
1 1/3 cups quick cooking grits
1/2   cup grated Parmesan
1/2   teaspoon salt
2   tablespoons butter, melted
1   (8-ounce) package cream cheese, softened
1   tablespoon half-and-half
1/2   cup grated Italian cheese blend
1   teaspoon dried chopped parsley
1/2   pound cooked, peeled and deveined shrimp, coarsely chopped
1/2   cup grated Cheddar cheese

Preheat oven to 400 degrees.

Bring broth to a rolling boil in a large saucepan. Slowly stir in grits and return to a boil. Cover, reduce heat and simmer for 5 minutes or until grits are thickened, stirring occasionally. Stir in Parmesan and salt; remove from heat. Spoon grits into a greased 9 x 13-inch baking pan. Cover and chill at least 2 hours or until firm.

Unmold grits onto a large cutting board. Cut into circles using a 2-inch round fluted cookie cutter. Brush a large jelly-roll pan with melted butter. Place grit rounds on the greased pan. Bake for 15 minutes; turn grits and bake 45 minutes longer. Set aside. Up unto this point the recipe may be made ahead. Cover and refrigerate grit rounds until ready to top with shrimp mixture.

Preheat broiler. To prepare shrimp topping, combine cream cheese and half-and-half in a large mixing bowl; stirring until smooth. Stir in Italian cheese, parsley and shrimp. Place grit rounds on a large baking sheet and top each evenly with shrimp mixture. Sprinkle Cheddar over tops and broil 5 minutes or until lightly browned and heated through.

DESTRUCTION

On August 29, 2005 the eye of Hurricane Katrina brought 150 MPH winds and a 25 foot tidal surge to the area... *a 25 foot wall of water.*

RECONSTRUCTION

PROFITS FROM THE SALES OF **SAVORING SLIDELL** WILL BE USED TO HELP CONSTRUCT A PUBLIC PLAZA NEAR CITY HALL, SIMILAR TO THE ONE PICTURED BELOW.

PHOTO BY JOHN MONTELEPRE, COURTESY OF JAN SMITH STUMPF.

Immediately following Hurricane Katrina, Slidellians began rebuilding homes, businesses, and lives. They will never forget what was lost, but are proud of what was gained: strength to meet any obstacle, pride in new found optimism and joy for the new families that have moved to the area.

A new five lane, state-of-the-art bridge now connects Slidell to New Orleans.

Bayou Bonfouca

PHOTO COURTESY OF SHAWN MACOMBER

Bayou Bonfouca

The Bayou Bonfouca area is known affectionately by many as "Olde Town," a coin termed by Audrey Browne, long-time activist in its renovation. Many African Americans in this area refer to it as "Lincoln Park."

Whatever the name, the area has old time appeal and 21st century functionality. The quaint antique district adds to the charm and numerous restaurants add the flavor.

City Hall and the Municipal Auditorium are in Olde Town. Many of the old buildings have been renovated for various professional businesses. The Olde Town Association works tirelessly to keep businesses open and thriving. Families (many multi-generational) reside in the area's neighborhoods, with majestic old trees, parks and a variety of architectural styles that have made the neighborhoods some of the more desirable in Slidell.

GATEWAY TO THE GARDEN
WATERCOLOR + INK
BY PINK LAGRANGE

HIDDEN IN THE WOODS
WATERCOLOR BY CINDY STRECKER

Gumbo des Herbs

3   bunches turnip greens
3   bunches mustard greens
3   bunches spinach
2   bunches beet tops
2   bunches radish tops
2   small heads green cabbage, coarsely cut
3   heads leaf lettuce, chopped
3   bunches sorrel, washed and stemmed
1/2   pound salt pork, diced
2-3   slices ham, diced
4   slices bacon, diced
    Salt and black pepper, to taste
    Hot cooked rice
    Cooked chicken, deboned and shredded, optional

Fill a stockpot about half full of cold water; bring to a boil. Wash well and stem turnip greens, mustard greens, spinach, beet tops and radish tops. Add all greens to the stockpot, then add cabbage, lettuce and sorrel; cook until all ingredients are tender.

In a skillet, over medium heat, brown salt pork, ham and bacon. Add meat and drippings to greens. Season with salt and pepper to taste and continue cooking over medium heat, covered, until mixture reaches the consistency of thick gumbo.

Serve over hot cooked rice and top with shredded chicken, if desired.

Note: This is a very old, and treasured, family recipe. Sorrell may be grown easily in the garden or in a container. If it is unavailable, add the juice of half a lemon to add the tart "bite" the dish needs.

The Slidell Feed and Seed, a multi-generational family business, has been providing plants and seeds to local garden lovers for years.

This landmark building, The Ice House, once provided ice for individuals, fishermen and other businesses, but has housed numerous other commercial endeavors within her walls throughout the years.

WHO LOVES A GARDEN

Who loves a garden

Finds within his soul, life's whole

He hears the anthem of the soil

While ingrates toil:

And sees beyond his little sphere

The waving fronds of heaven, clear.

—LOUISE SEYMOUR JONES

TAKING IT ALL IN
PHOTO BY SHARON DELONG

Slidell Cleaners, a familiar landmark on the corner of Robert and First Streets, was established in 1929 by Joseph Johnson and his wife, Rhoda Parks Johnson. All dry and wet cleaning was done by hand in wooden tubs and wooden buckets. In 1982, they turned the business over to their nephew, Eric DuBuisson and his wife, Mary, who continued to provide the same careful and caring service to their customers through 2005 when Hurricane Katrina destroyed everything in the store. Today, the building houses DuBuisson Galleries. Artists display their works, art workshops are held for young and old and the gallery may be rented for parties and other special events.

Savoring Slidell

The Bayou Bonfouca area boasts several excellent restaurants. There aren't many places in the country where you can sit back, relax and dine with a serene waterfront setting stretched out before you. Nathan's, built on Bayou Bonfouca, is one of them. Its docking facilities invite guests to pull up by car or by boat. Either way, they'll be treated to delicious food, scenic views and a warm, friendly atmosphere.

Christopher Case is the chef at Christopher's on Carey (the former Victorian Tea Room). According to his parents, John and Brenda Case, Christopher had an inclination toward the culinary arts at an early age. He attended Delgado

Roasted Eggplant and Brie Soup

3	eggplants
	Olive oil
	Salt and black pepper
8	whole cloves garlic
1	small yellow onion, chopped
3	ribs celery, chopped
1	green pepper, seeded and chopped
1	cup white wine
2	quarts chicken or vegetable stock
1	bunch fresh thyme sprigs, tied with butcher's twine
2	bay leaves
1	(8-ounce) round of Brie, diced
2	cups heavy cream

Preheat oven to 400 degrees.

Cut eggplants in half lengthwise and place on baking sheets, meat side up. Drizzle each with olive oil and sprinkle with salt and pepper. Roast eggplant in oven for 30-45 minutes or until golden browned and meat is soft to the touch. Remove from oven and set aside to cool.

In a soup pot or Dutch oven heat enough olive oil to coat the bottom of the pot. Add whole garlic and sauté on medium high until they begin to brown very lightly. Add onion, celery and pepper and sauté until soft. Add white wine and stir until mixture comes to a boil.

Add stock, thyme and bay leaves and bring mixture to a simmer. Scoop cooled eggplant out of skin and add to soup pot; simmer about 45 minutes. Add Brie and stir until melted.

Remove thyme twigs and bay leaves. Puree mixture with an immersion blender until smooth. If using a stand blender or food processor, do it in small batches and add back to pot. After blending, bring mixture to simmer. Stir in heavy cream and adjust seasonings before serving.

CREOLE TOMATOES
PASTEL BY MARY PAT LANDRY

Culinary School and Johnson and Whales Culinary Institute in Charlotte, North Carolina. Now he's back home and a respected member of the culinary scene.

The site of present day Palmetto's on the Bayou Restaurant can be considered the birthplace of Slidell. Early settlers caught the ferry there, known as Robert's Landing, and sailed to New Orleans to sell and trade their wares at the French Market.

The original train station was built just a few feet from that ferry landing.

Today, the view from the bayou at Palmetto's is spectacular. Beautiful decks highlight the natural beauty of the setting and owners Kirk Dunbar and Duffy Ramirez provide delicious, unique food and live music. Sunday Brunch is a "must"!

PALMETTOS ON THE BAYOU
ACRYLIC BY JUDITH CANULETTE

LOUISIANA SWAMP BEAUTY
PASTEL BY JEAN M. LAJAUNIE

ALLEN AND KATHY LITTLE

Allen and Kathleen Little, two remarkable patrons of the arts, purchased their home at 106 West Hall Ave, an original *American Creosote* house, in 1970. (The structure was built and designed by a Mr. Hersey, the Creosote Plant Manager.) Since then, the Littles continue to expand and update the home, now known as Chateau Bleu. In 1974 they established their successful catering business with events held on and off the premises.

The Littles have been active in the community in a variety of areas. Allen won many awards with the Slidell Jaycees, was chairman of the Slidell Bicentennial Commission, founding chairman of the Slidell Museum, a member of the original Mayor's Commission on the Arts, a board member and past president of the Slidell Little Theatre, and captain of the Krewe of Perseus.

Kathy taught home economics at Pearl River High School and she and Allen reigned as Queen and King of Krewe de la Boutte Dominique. A member of the Slidell Jaynes and the Krewe of Perseus, she was Queen of Perseus and St. Patrick's Day Queen.

She and Allen enjoy traveling and have hosted numerous European tours.

CHATEAU BLEU
PEN & INK SANDY LINDSAY

LANGIAPPE

Garden Tip:
Prune ever-blooming roses back about a third of their height in late August or early September.

GOD'S GARDEN

The kiss of the sun for pardon
The song of the birds for mirth-
One is nearer God's heart in a garden
Than anywhere else on earth.

DOROTHY FRANCES GURNEY

PHOTO COURTESY OF THE STONEBRIDGE GARDEN CLUB

The Stonebridge Garden Club is a small, relatively new garden club to the Slidell area. Founded in March 2009, they strive to keep the entrance to Stonebridge Estates maintained and attractive.

Divinity Candy

2 cups granulated sugar
1/2 cup water
1/2 light corn syrup
1/8 teaspoon salt
2 egg whites
1/2 teaspoon vanilla
1/2 teaspoon almond extract
25 walnut halves

Butter a large baking sheet and set aside.

In a large, heavy saucepan, combine sugar, water and corn syrup. Heat, stirring, until sugar dissolves. Boil, stirring constantly, until syrup forms a hard ball when dropped in cold water.

In a mixing bowl, add salt and egg whites and beat mixture quickly until stiff peaks form.

Slowly add syrup to egg white mixture while beating vigorously. (It might be helpful for one person to mix and someone else add the syrup.)

Beat until candy thickens and begins to lose its sheen. Stir in flavorings and quickly shape with a spoon into large pieces; drop on the prepared sheet and top each piece with a walnut half.

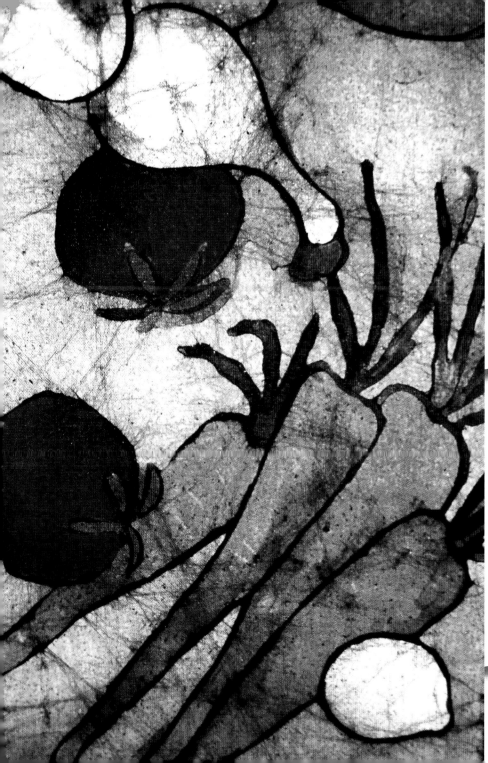

Sweet Potatoes Divine

3	large sweet potatoes, peeled and grated (raw)
1	cup granulated sugar
1/2	cup brown sugar
2	eggs lightly beaten
2	tablespoons melted butter
1/4	teaspoon baking powder
2/3	cup evaporated milk
1	teaspoon vanilla
1	teaspoon cinnamon
1/2	teaspoon allspice
1/2	teaspoon nutmeg

Preheat oven to 375 degrees. Lightly grease a large baking dish and set aside.

Add sweet potatoes to a large mixing bowl. Add remaining ingredients and mix well. Spoon mixture into prepared baking dish. Bake for 30 minutes or until potatoes are tender.

This wonderful hot dish is delicious served alongside a pork roast or roasted turkey or chicken.

Corn & Crawfish Soup

8	tablespoons butter
1	large onion, chopped
1	(12-ounce) cans evaporated milk
2	(10.75-ounce) cans cream of potato soup
1	(10.75-ounce) can cream of celery soup
1	(10.75-ounce) can cheddar cheese soup
2	(15-ounce) cans cream-style corn
1	pound crawfish tails
	Salt and black pepper, to taste
	Tony Chachere's Seasoning, to taste

In a large, heavy saucepan over medium heat, melt butter. Sauté onion until opaque, about 3 to 4 minutes.

Add milk, soups, corn and crawfish tails; stir well to blend. Add seasonings to taste and simmer for about 20 minutes, or until hot through, but not boiling.

ANTIQUE ALLEY

"Antique Alley" on First Street in Slidell is a quaint place to shop, stroll, and meet friends for lunch. Browsing through the treasures of other people from earlier times stirs the imagination. In addition to being a great place to find the perfect antique nick-knack, it's also a great place to rekindle your own treasured memories.

Various businesses have occupied the buildings throughout the years. Old timers remember Patsy Folse's flower shop and Pomroy Lowry's interior decorating shop. Cornibe's Barber Shop has been in the same location for decades. It is a place of memories and a place to find the perfect something for yourself or someone else.

ANTIQUE ALLEY
OIL BY LYNDA A. DONALDSON

Sunny Citrus Salad

1 pint creamy cottage cheese
1 (3-ounce) package orange –flavored gelatin mix
1 small can Mandarin orange segments, drained
1 (8-ounce) container non-dairy whipped topping, slightly thawed

Add cottage cheese to a large mixing bowl. Stir in dry gelatin and mix well. Fold in orange segments and then whipped topping. Spoon into a glass bowl or serving dish and chill well before serving.

This light and tangy salad is not your grandmother's congealed salad! It's a different take on an old favorite.

Quick Buttermilk Biscuits

1 cup solid shortening
4 cups self-rising flour
1 3/4 cups buttermilk

Preheat oven to 425 degrees. Lightly grease two baking sheets and set aside.

Using a pastry blender or two forks, cut shortening into flour until the mixture is crumbly. Add buttermilk, stirring just until dry ingredients are moistened.

Turn dough out onto a lightly floured surface and knead 4 to 5 times. Pat or roll dough to 3/4-inch thickness. Cut with 1 1/2-inch biscuit cutter and place on prepared pans.

Bake 12 to 14 minutes until lightly browned.

No southern breakfast is complete without hot biscuits. These are quick, easy and tasty—the perfect combination!

COMMUNITY PARKS

Slidell has several beautifully maintained parks and recreation areas. They contain nature trails, ball parks, gyms for youth and adult sports teams, bayous to stroll along, benches for sitting and reading, picnic tables for groups and family gatherings, open spaces with amphitheaters for concerts as well as iris gardens for quiet reflection. Their names reflect the history of our town: Memorial Park to honor veterans, Fritchie Park to honor the family who donated the land for the park, John Slidell Park for its namesake, and Heritage Park to honor their ancestors.

In Old Town there is a small park adjoining the Municipal Auditorium that is named for Dr. John Keller Griffith. Dr. Griffith not only served the residents as a doctor, but also as a political leader and community activist.

Dr. Griffith was born in East Baton Rouge Parish is 1882 and began practicing medicine in Slidell in 1910. He was elected to the United States House of Representatives; was founder of the Slidell Lions Club, active in the American Legion and a director of the Bank of Slidell. He and his family lived in a home at 512 Teddy Avenue.

He died in 1942 and is buried in Slidell's Greenwood Cemetery.

SHARON DELONG

SLIDELL COMMUNITY PLAYGROUND HERITAGE PARK
PHOTO BY KIM BERGERON, DIRECTOR OF CULTURAL AFFAIRS, CITY OF SLIDELL

Orlando Magic's Chris Duhon, who first moved to Slidell when he was nine years old, considers Slidell his hometown.

An honor graduate of Salmen High School, he received several academic and basketball awards including McDonald's All-American, Louisiana Mr. Basketball, and Gatorade All-American.

He attended Duke University in Durham, NC on a basketball scholarship. Chris was an intricate member of the 2001 NCAA Men's Basketball Champions as a member of the Duke University Blue Devils. He graduated in May 2004 with a Bachelor of Science degree in Sociology and a certificate in Business Marketing.

Chris was drafted by the NBA Chicago Bulls in July 2004 and played for the Bulls for four years. He played for the New York Knicks for two years before joining the Orlando Magics.

In August 2005, Chris Duhon established a hurricane relief fund with the Stand Tall Foundation to provide aid to of Slidell, which was devastated by Hurricane Katrina.

His philanthropic activities were recognized in 2005 when he was the recipient of the Sporting News' Good Guy Award. He was also honored by the NBA with the Community Assist Award in 2007.

The foundation has been active in developing projects to assist the community in many ways. He returns to Slidell annually and partners with Feed the Children for his annual Thanksgiving food giveaway for families in need.

Chris also created the Stand Tall Foundation Scholarship which awards five $5,000 scholarships to graduating seniors in St. Tammany Parish Public Schools who have demonstrated outstanding academics, leadership abilities and their commitment to the community. He also returns home annually for a charity golf tournament which serves as a fund-raiser for the foundation.

Chris partners with his high school coach, Jay Carlin, for the Chris Duhon Basketball Camp. The five-day camp is designed for boys and girls ages 7-15 and focuses on fundamentals of basketball such as dribbling, shooting, passing, rebounding and defense.

A WIDE VARIETY OF SPORTS ARE PLAYED YEAR ROUND. FROM SOCCER TO SWIMMING, FROM T-BALL TO ADULT BASKETBALL, SLIDELL MEN, WOMEN AND CHILDREN ENJOY ORGANIZED AND IMPROMPTU SPORTS. PARENTS COACH, CHEER AND SUPPORT THE TEAMS AS YOUNG AND OLD LEARN SPORTSMANSHIP AND TEAMWORK. THIS PHOTO, COURTESY OF DR. DARRELL BLALOCK, SHOWS HIS SON, CRAIG, COACHING HIS GRANDSON, CADE.

THE SLIDELL GARDEN CLUB

The Slidell Garden Club, founded on September 28, 1959 with 24 charter members has worked to preserve the history and enhance the beauty of this, The Camellia City. Through their projects, such as a sunflower growing contest for fourth graders and participation in the City of Slidell "Christmas under the Stars," they strive to be an active part of the community. They maintain the MIA Memorial monument at Memorial Park and send boxes of needed items to US servicemen and women. As educators in the art of flower arranging and gardening, they enhance the beauty of the community.

Through their teas and meetings they strive to keep the art of Southern entertaining alive. By encouraging the growth and conservation of natural resources, they work to leave this spot on earth better than they found it.

The women of the Slidell Garden Club dedicate this book "to the people of Slidell: those who came before us, those who are with us now, and those who will come after us to continue our work. "

Garden Tip
Irises like to keep their feet wet.

Colorful Cucumber Stacks

1	loaf sliced cocktail bread
1/4	cup mayonnaise
1-2	cucumbers, peeled
2	small red onions, peeled
	Lemon pepper seasoning, to taste

Spread each slice of cocktail bread lightly with mayonnaise and place on a large baking sheet.

Thinly slice cucumbers and onions, using a mandolin (preferred) or very sharp knife. Place a slice of cucumber in the center of each prepared bread slice. Separate onions into small single rings. Add one ring to each of the bread slices, placing it to encircle the cucumber slice.

Sprinkle tops lightly with lemon pepper and serve immediately or cover with plastic wrap and refrigerate until ready to serve.

Note: These lovely canapés take a little "hands-on" time and effort but are worth it. Practice will help in selecting the right size onions to fit perfectly around the cucumber slice for a dramatic presentation.

Recipe for Cleaning Silver
from Catherine Felder

1/3 cup Spic and Span powder
hot water

Place a sheet or two of aluminum foil in the bottom and up the sides of a sink or a large plastic pan. Pour Spic & Span on the foil. Add about 4 - 6" very hot water. Place your silver on the foil and let it sit for about 3 minutes.

Remove-and admire your beautiful shiny silver. If it is not to your standards, place back in pan for an additional 5 minutes.

LOUISIANA IRIS
WATERCOLOR BY BARBARA GAINES

Garden Spot Nursery

A Passion for Plants

Jan Breaux and her brother, David Parr, inherited the same "passion for plants" that led their parents, Louis and Margaret, to found Garden Spot Nursery in 1964. David's son, David Jr., has become the third generation of the family to inherit this passion that has identified the family for more than four decades.

Under Jan and David's management, the business has expanded to become one of the largest full-service retail garden centers in St. Tammany Parrish. Customers from as far away as Houma, Baton Rouge, and communities along the Gulf Coast have learned that Garden Spot Nursery is their one-stop center for residential and commercial landscaping and irrigation. Set amidst four acres of trees, shrubs, pottery, and yard art is a 6,500-square foot showroom building, awash in color from flowering plants ranging from hibiscus, jasmine, and plumeria to pitcher plants and herbs.

"We, as a city, have gone through so much together since the devastation of Katrina," Jan states. "I feel that we are here to help people beautify their homes inside and out. Sometimes, the smell of a flower, the sound of water bubbling, or a simple stroll among the gardens can have a calming effect on what life throws our way."

BLUE HERON
WATERCOLOR BY LUCY BAND

SLIDELL MEMORIAL HOSPITAL

YOUR HOSPITAL FOR LIFE

It came as little surprise that Slidell Memorial Hospital's 50th anniversary of serving the people of St. Tammany Parish coincided with the healthcare facility's being named to the list of "Best Places to Work" by New Orleans City Business magazine. The vision for the hospital to become nationally recognized for superior quality was achieved while, at the same time, a positive work environment for its healthcare professionals was created and has been recognized as among the best places to work in the area. The anniversary celebration in 2009 marked a half-century of service to the community through its commitment to compassionate care and a patient-centered culture.

When Slidell Memorial Hospital first opened its doors in 1959, the facility was on a recently paved two-lane Gause Boulevard which, at that time, was considered "out in the country." As Slidell grew over the years, so too did Slidell Memorial Hospital evolve into a leader in advanced healthcare technology.

WORLD CLASS CARE IN A NEIGHBORHOOD SETTING

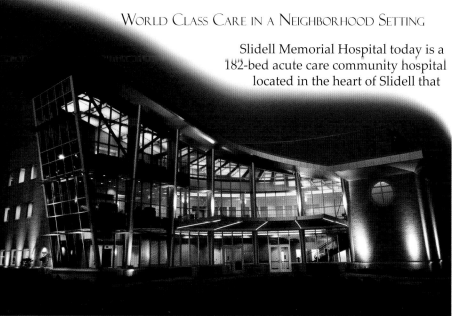

Slidell Memorial Hospital today is a 182-bed acute care community hospital located in the heart of Slidell that provides access to the latest treatments and technology administered by expert physicians. A dedicated team of more than 1,000 healthcare professionals and 296 physicians provide high quality care to meet the needs of the people of eastern St. Tammany Parish and parts of Mississippi. Through the years, the hospital has earned the respect and trust of the community through a series of "firsts" that established the reputation of Slidell Memorial as a center of excellence.

- Slidell Memorial brought to the north shore of Lake Pontchartrain the first Neonatal Intensive Care Unit.
- The hospital's cardiac specialists performed the first open heart surgery on the north shore.
- The north shore's first brain surgery was performed by specialists at SMH.
- Slidell Memorial was the first to bring the most advanced imaging equipment to the area.
- Slidell Memorial's orthopedic specialists are among only a handful in the region to offer anterior hip replacement surgery using a Hana™ Hip and Knee Arthroplasty Table, one of just 100 in use across the country.
- More recently, SMH brought the first Image Guided Radiation Therapy system to Louisiana, at the time, only the eleventh in the United States and the fourth at a non-teaching institution.
- Slidell Memorial has recently introduced High Dose Brachytherapy, another advancement in cancer treatment that significantly reduces the length of treatment for certain cancer patients.

LEADING THE WAY IN CANCER TREATMENT

An estimated 22,000 people in Louisiana this year will be diagnosed with some form of cancer. To offer unparalleled treatment for this disease, SMH broke ground in 2009 on a new regional cancer center that brings hope as well as healing to cancer patients and their families in the community. And as the only community-owned, not-for-profit hospital in eastern St. Tammany Parish, Slidell Memorial proudly stands on the threshold of becoming one of the most advanced regional cancer centers in the South.

The new SMHRCC centralizes all of SMH's current cancer treatments and cancer-specific diagnostic equipment, providing patients convenient access to outpatient services and a wide range of resources. Drawing patients from the entire Gulf South region, the SMHRCC's outstanding specialists and nurses utilize the most advanced treatment and technology to diagnose, treat, and rehabilitate patients.

The National Institutes of Cancer projects 98 percent of all cancers can be most effectively treated if the patient is close to home in a center that can provide adequate treatment. Slidell Memorial Hospital's Regional Cancer Center negates the long distance travel previously necessary to receive that quality care. Being near family and friends plays an important role in patient recovery and healing.

Looking Toward the Future

In a continuous effort to bring high-quality healthcare to Slidell, SMH has several patient care initiatives in progress. A recently completed addition to MD Imaging, SMH's outpatient imaging facility, includes a Women's Imaging Center, which marries the most advanced imaging technology with a relaxing, spa-like atmosphere. In addition, the SMHRCC is striving to become an integral part of cancer research. The center is working on establishing a variety of partnerships to bring the benefits of clinical trials to its patients.

In April 2011, SMH received approval to dedicate a bond renewal to the construction of a new expanded Emergency Department facility on Twelfth Street that will also house up to 36 new inpatient private rooms. This project will allow more people to access healthcare services with shorter wait times.

The hospital is focused on another patient care initiative: to become a Primary Stroke Center through Joint Commission Certification. This program will ensure all patients appropriate, standardized stroke care using best practice guidelines, from rapid diagnosis, treatment and rehabilitation, to educating the community on how to recognize and respond to a stroke for the best results possible. Additionally, infants, children and even expectant mothers will benefit from a strategic partnership with LSU Pediatric Cardiology Services. With plans to house a

clinic facility on the SMH campus in the future, LSU Pediatric Cardiology Services adds a new dimension to patient services here in Slidell.

Neighbors Helping Neighbors

The dedicated and caring professionals at Slidell Memorial Hospital are actively involved in numerous healthcare initiatives that offer their services far beyond the confines of the hospital. Ever responsive to the needs of a growing community, Slidell Memorial sponsors community events such as free or reduced-cost health screenings to the public. Monthly prenatal and parenting education classes and community support groups help educate and support parents in raising their families. The SMH Women's Health Alliance conducts a seminar featuring health screenings followed by lunch, a presentation, and a fashion show. Volunteers ranging in age from sixteen to over 80 give thousands of hours to their community, serving countless patients, visitors, and medical personnel in numerous ways throughout the year.

These and other programs sponsored by Slidell Memorial Hospital are part of the hospital's commitment to compassionate care and improving the quality of life in the local community.

BAYOU LIBERTY

Rooted In Liberté

By Charlotte Lowry Collins

Bayou Liberty, originally Liberté, has always been a hidden gem. The only way to view the area is by boat. When I was growing up, boaters had to wait for our slow, hand-cranked bridge to open in order to enter or leave the bayou. Most of the speed boats opted for the wide banks of Bayou Bonfouca, or Lake Pontchartrian. Even its replacement, a beloved, quirky, cable swing bridge that frequently broke, discouraged many boaters. After Hurricane Katrina, a new "high-rise" bridge was inevitable.

I became compelled to collect the history of this area before it changed too drastically. As we rode up and down the bayou waiting for residents to return, we realized time was further deteriorating vacant homes. I fervently began to capture the way things were through photography. Luckily, I was able to preserve this imagery before we lost those that were razed.

One thing I did not anticipate was the rich history and captivating family stories waiting to be shared. Long before Slidell was even a whistle stop, this community was thriving as a source of refuge for Native American, French, Spanish, Creole, Acadian, African and Caribbean cultures as well as the latecomers, the English and American residents.

Recording these stories from our elders became a passion for me. Through a grant from Kennesaw State University, colleagues and students visited to help us rebuild and compile my research into a hand bound "Artist's Book," which I bring to local organizations and groups. Before long, I joined forces with others passionate about our history through the Olde Towne Arts Center, Guardians of Slidell History, St. Tammany Parish Commission on Cultural Affairs, and the Lake Pontchartrain Basin Maritime Museum for public exhibitions.

Bayou Liberty 1
Etching by Mary Ellen Davidson
Courtesy of Cindy and Jerry Negueloua

SHELL MIDDEN

By Charlotte Lowry Collins

Imagine the history behind this raised bank. These shells are evidence of an ancient activity. Each time I pass this shell midden, or mound, I find myself drawn to it, transfixed. Of course, you can only reach this spot by boat, as it is the first high ground amidst the marsh as you come up the bayou from Lake Pontchartrain.

The white shells, or bivalves, sparkle in contrast to the rich, black mud, and dark green palmettos. They were collected and opened on this spot by Native Americans who first called this area home. Exactly what all of these shells were used for is unknown, but I picture them used as bait for crabbing or fishing. I also imagine they had quite a technique for harvesting soft shell crabs.

The early historians recorded over 70 villages in the Bayou Liberty area. Today, they are known as Chahta. Europeans began settling in the area and interacting with the Chahta. They called this community Bonfouca, Creole for "good people." Oddly enough, it is located on Bayou Liberty, not Bayou Bonfouca. The Chahta had developed techniques for hunting, fishing, farming, basket weaving, herbal

SHELL MIDDENS—PHOTO BY CHARLOTTE LOWRY COLLINS

remedies, and many other vital resources.

Chahta knowledge of the regional resources, and their generosity in sharing that knowledge, helped the Europeans and Creoles to survive many hardships in the early 1800s.

PHOTO OF ELVIDGE DUMAS DOUCETTE
COURTESY OF ALICE D.TWILLIE

St. Genevieve's Church

Madame Anatole Cousin, the former Camille Pichon, built St. Genevieve Church in 1852 on the extensive land holdings of the Cousin family, known as Bonfouca. The Cousins were refugees of the French Revolution. She named the church in honor of her mother, Genevieve Dubuisson. Originally, services were attended by the Pichon family and the family slaves.

The church's past is also linked to Abbe' Adrian Rouquette, a classical poet, a native Creole priest, and a missionary among the Choctaw Indians, who inhabited the area long before European settlers. The nephew of Anatole Cousin, he offered mass at St. Genevieve for the family and his Choctaw converts.

Eventually the land and church were donated to the archdiocese of the Roman Catholic Church. Over the years, buildings were added and expanded. Then, in 2005, Hurricane Katrina destroyed much of the complex. Now rebuilt, St. Genevieve serves its diverse congregation, who work, worship and live nearby as they have for generations.

Chapel on the Bayou
Photo By Beth Alexander Galyon

Doucette Family

PHOTO: DAUGHTER ALBERTINE AND ELVIDGE DOUCETTE, WIFE OF JOSEPH DOUCETTE, WITH GREAT GRAND-DAUGHTER MARGARET DOUCETTE-DAVIS—COURTESY OF ALICE D.TWILLIE

Captain Edgar Doucette, an early settler in the Bayou Pacquet area of Slidell, obtained more than three hundred acres of farm and timber land on the bayou through the Zenon-Mellon Land Grant.

Alice Twillie, a former librarian at Florida Avenue Elementary School, is his great, great granddaughter. She notes: "Captain Edgar was owner and operator of schooners that brought lumber to New Orleans and brought back goods and foods, including ice cream packed in dry ice. "His sons, her great grandfather, Joseph Doucette, and Walter and Edward Doucette, worked on the schooners and later in the shipyard. "My father, Albert, recalled traveling across Lake Pontchartrain in a schooner to deliver and pick up goods with his grandfather, Joseph."

Alice Twillie is now retired and living in the Bayou Liberty area.

Snippet from the Past

Captain Charles Butler McVay III and his ship, the *Indianapolis*, were assigned to carry the atomic bomb from San Francisco to Tinian Island in the Pacific. The bomb was dropped on Hiroshima and sealed the fate of the Japanese Empire ending World War II. After successfully delivering the bomb, he departed Tinian Island on route to Leyte. His ship was sunk by a Japanese submarine. Almost 900 men lost their lives; some killed by sharks. It was the greatest loss of life of any American ship disaster in World War II.

Captain McVay was court martialed after the war for endangering his ship by failing to steer a zigzag course. He was the only captain court martialed for events leading to losing a ship. He was court martialed to cover up a long list of mistakes made by the Navy. He may have been court martialed to cover up the fact that the U.S. Intelligence had deciphered the complicated Ultra Code that the Japanese used. The Navy may have known that there was danger in his path, but chose not to divulge it, thus letting the Japanese know their code was broken. That fact was not made public for over forty years.

He lived in Slidell, on Bayou Liberty from 1956 until his wife's death in 1961. He continued to own the property until his death in 1968. His ashes were scattered on Bayou Liberty

In 2001 Congress exonerated Captain McVay from all wrongdoing. He is considered by those that have studied him, a martyr and American Hero.

—BY JOHN CASE

A Creole Cottage

As you meander down the slow, brown waters of Bayou Liberty, allow all of your senses to embrace this, the oldest part of our community. You'll see Creole cottages, the Tranquility Plantation, and homes that at one time were summer retreats for New Orleanians. Moss hanging from the oaks intensifies the sense of quiet. You can almost hear the Choctaw Indians and Creole people sharing basket making, clay making and fishing tips.

Hear the names Pichon, Galatas, Dubuisson or Cousin being whispered. They inhabited this area for generations. Smell the pun gent odor of fish and the spicy odor of crawfish being boiled in a large, outdoor pot. Feel the warmth of the sun and the cool of the shade. Wave to the people passing in pirogues being paddled or motor boats ambling along. Enjoy the sounds of egrets, frogs and the abundance of wildlife. Savor and enjoy this piece of history.

The Creole cottage pictured below once belonged to Etienne Galatas and then became the home to his son, Salvadore "Jack" and Albertine Galatas, and their son, Steve. The Narcisse and Doucette families share a revered ancestor, Captain Edgar Doucette, known as "Capitaine." Bayou Narcisse runs off Bayou Liberty and joins with Bayou Paul before making a full circle back to Bayou Liberty. These bayous are barely navigable today, even by pirogue, but provide a home for many of our waterfowl, alligators, and beautiful spider lilies. Prior to Katrina it held one of the largest beaver dams along Bayou Liberty.

PHOTO OF NARCISSE HOME—PHOTO BY CHARLOTTE LOWRY COLLINS

Francois Cousin Home

Owned and Restored by William and Pomeroy Lowry

As you pass the front of this Creole house, one senses the history that infuses the entire property. The Francois Cousin Home has been restored by owners, William and Pomeroy Lowry. An interior designer with a penchant for history, Pomeroy suspected the home dated back before the Civil War. However, carbon testing has proved the home to be circa 1787-9, older than the Louisiana Purchase. It is possibly the oldest home in St. Tammany Parish, and is on the National Register of Historic Places.

"My father learned that the man who originally built the home, Francois Cousin, was the son of a French Naval officer. Cousin was sent to settle the new French territory, and received a Spanish grant for this property with magnificent oaks," explains the Lowry's daughter Charlotte Collins.

As a friend of the Chahta, Cousin learned where the superior veins of clay lay as well as the native brick-making techniques. His bricks helped rebuild New Orleans after the great fires in 1788 and 1794.

Cousin owned schooners and had slaves, and brought goods back and forth to New Orleans by way of Bayou St. John. He built this home from hand-made bricks and hand-hewn cypress, using the historic brick-between-post architecture.

Cousin and his sons, Anatole, Terence and Francois Jr., owned several homes on this and neighboring bayous, including the ones known as Tranquility Plantation and Camp Salmen.

LOWRY/COUSIN HOME
PHOTO BY CHARLOTTE LOWRY COLLINS

TRANQUILITY PLANTATION

Tranquility is one of many beautiful mansions situated on Bayou Liberty. Access to these homes is limited and can best be viewed from a boat ride on the bayou. Tranquility was built on an original land grant in 1803 by Francois DuBuisson. In 1840 the land was acquired by Terrence Cousin who erected a structure around the pioneer structure. Today it is privately owned.

TRANQUILITY PLANTATION
OIL BY BRUCE HUME

Gardner and Ronnie Kole

"The essence of all art is to have pleasure in giving pleasure."

MIKHAIL BARYSHNIKOV

Nestled on the banks of Bayou Liberty, Chateau Kole, home of Gardner and Ronnie Kole, has been the site of countless galas. Their signature event, Jazz on the Bayou supports Louisiana Easter Seals and STARC and will soon celebrate its 20th year. At the annual benefit, guests sample fabulous wines and delicious food from famous chefs while bidding on auction items and enjoying live jazz.

This celebration of food, art, music and friends was born years earlier from Gardner's desire to enhance the city of Slidell by sponsoring musical, dance and theatrical performances and by providing educational funding for the arts in schools.

When Gardner arrived in Slidell in 1951, as the young bride of Pete Schneider (St. Joe Brick), she took an active role in promoting charitable causes. She became a charter member of Slidell Junior Auxiliary and an active member of Ozone Camellia Club. At that time Slidell lacked an arts community. It was their passion for the arts that led to the creation of the Slidell Performing Arts Guild and the infusion of world class music and dance into Slidell. After Pete's untimely death she continued their good work.

As a skilled dancer and accomplished dance instructor, Gardner appreciated the importance of exposing children to the arts. Consequently, many of the Guild's early programs involved bringing musicians and dancers to the schools. Fundraising was essential to support these programs, and Gardner loved to entertain. However, to raise substantial funds, she needed a big name---and one willing to donate his time and talent to the cause. Therefore, for one of these events, she contacted world-renowned jazz pianist Ronnie Kole and asked if he'd play. He agreed.

Gardner shares the story: "Everyone was there for the benefit, and it started to rain. We all grabbed everything and ran inside. Ronnie played for us...I enjoyed it so much that I told him he'd have to play for me every time I passed and tapped him on the shoulder." They wed in 1984, and their marriage of music and dance, along with a mutual love of entertaining, was the beginning of their shared philanthropy.

Together they've travelled the world as ambassadors for our music, our culture, and our people. Throughout the years, proceeds from the Kole's fundraisers have supported not only the Slidell Performing Arts Guild (now the Slidell Symphony Society), but also the Slidell Commission on the Arts, Slidell Little Theatre and dozens of other worthy causes. Gardner and Ronnie Kole, gracious hostess and world-class musician, were instrumental in the establishment of the Slidell arts community. Through their support, they continue to enrich the lives of its citizens of all ages.

Mandarin Orange Cake

Cake:
1   (18-ounce) box moist yellow cake mix
1/2   cup vegetable oil
1/2   cup water
2   eggs
1   can Mandarin oranges

Preheat oven to 350 degrees. Grease and flour a 9 x 13-inch baking pan and set aside.

Combine cake mix, oil and water and blend well with electric mixer. Drain juice from oranges and add to cake mixture, mixing well. Fold in oranges and mix briefly on low speed to incorporate them into the batter. Pour into prepared pan and bake for 30-35 minutes.

Remove from oven and cool before adding Frosting.

Frosting:
1   (20-ounce) can crushed pineapple
1   (3.4-ounce) package instant vanilla pudding mix
1   can Mandarin oranges, drained and chopped
1   (12-ounce) carton frozen whipped topping, thawed

Mix pineapple, with liquid, and pudding mix until well-blended. (If pineapple is in natural juice, do not use the full amount of liquid.) Fold whipped topping into pineapple mixture and add chopped oranges. Spread frosting mixture over cooled cake; cover and refrigerate until ready to serve. For best results, make cake a day ahead of serving.

Camp Salmen

CAMP SALMEN
PHOTO BY CHARLOTTE LOWRY COLLINS

Located on scenic Bayou Liberty, Camp Salmen Nature Park served as the major trading post in the Bayou Liberty region for over a century. It is also a rich ecological endowment of native landscapes and an unusually diverse community of plants and animals, which make the Camp Salmen Nature Park a living museum.

Through federal and state funding, St. Tammany Parish Government purchased the 130-acre Camp Salmen property in 2004 to preserve the historical, cultural, biological and archaeological legacies and to transform it into a public recreational park. It is now open to the public, with a large pavilion, interpretive trails, and much more to come. Many Slidell campers have fond memories of their days there.

Dr. Robert Taylor, a former Scoutmaster of Troop 98, recalls the excitement of playing "Infiltration" at the camp. "We would divide into two teams and select an area for Base. One team would defend with our strongest flashlights and the other team would try to get into Base before we could lay a light on them," Dr. Taylor remembers.

"One night Base was established in a wide open area and nobody was able to get in. We had flashlight tagged and captured most of the opposing team but Jeff Roach was missing. Right about the time we decided to call it a night in comes Jeff, he had crawled on his belly through a patch of low brush…. before jumping up and running in the last few yards. However, we had the last laugh the next morning when we saw that he had been crawling through a field of poison ivy!"

Tom Collins recalls his days at Camp Salmen: "Over nearly six decades, tens of thousands of scouts spent some of their formative teenage years camping at Camp Salmen. Their collective experience produced a culture that has endured. For me, it was a real life adventure. The memory is old, but then again, so am I. It was the mid-fifties; I was a Cub Scout, and my Kenner based Cub Pack was on a weekend trip to Camp Salmen."

He continues: "Taking off alone through the underbrush, I felt at home and at peace on the bayou…Suddenly I found myself eye-to-eye with an adult boar with large tusks. His acceleration in my direction left no time to contemplate options, and my retreat was immediate and swift….One quick glance over my shoulder confirmed that I was about to lose this footrace," when he was able to climb 15 feet up a tree and wait as the boar gave a frustrated snort and left, northbound. Then he ran southbound to his Cub Scout companions and the safety of numbers.

CAMP SALMEN, SLIDELL, LA
OIL BY ESTER WYMAN

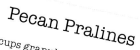

Pecan Pralines

2 cups granulated sugar
1 teaspoon baking soda
1 cup buttermilk
1/8 teaspoon salt
2 tablespoons butter
2 cups broken pecan pieces
1 teaspoon vanilla

In a large heavy saucepan, combine sugar, soda, buttermilk and salt. Cook over high heat for 5 minutes, stirring almost constantly. Scrape bottom of pan; add butter and pecans. Continue cooking about 5 minutes until candy reaches soft ball stage.

Remove from heat and add vanilla; cool slightly. Beat until creamy and drip quickly be tablespoons onto wax paper. Cool completely.

Garden Tip:

Trim or cut back your azaleas shortly after they bloom. The rest of the year they are forming blooms for the following spring.

This garden tip was provided by the Bayou Liberty Garden Club, the oldest garden club in the Slidell area. Founded in 1950 by Mrs. Eugene Bierhorst and Mrs. Leonard Elmer, the Bayou Liberty Garden Club has spent more than 60 years sharing their love of gardening with the Slidell community. They have adopted areas of the city to beautify, planted trees and flowers throughout the area and participated in flower arranging competitions.

Savoring Slidell

Pirogue Races

Armand "Junior" Pichon has been instrumental in maintaining the annual Pirogue Races on Bayou Liberty. It was Junior's grocery store on Bayou Liberty Road that was a Slidell landmark for several decades.

The first Pirogue Race was held in June 1951, sponsored by the Holy Name Society of St. Genevieve's Church. It was a fundraiser for the building of a new church. The winners were: Pete Syrenet, first place; Dave Pichon, second place; his grandson, Troy Holden, third place, and another grandson, "Junior" Pichon, fourth place.

Families looked forward to the races every year through 2010 when construction of the new church, destroyed by Hurricane Katrina, required the races to be on hold until June 2012. That will be the 60th race!

Whiskey Sour Punch

1 (6-ounce) can frozen orange juice concentrate, thawed
1 (6-ounce) can frozen lemonade concentrate, thawed
1 tablespoon angostura bitters
2 tablespoons sugar
2 (32-ounce) bottles club soda
1 or 2 packages whiskey sour mix, to taste
Maraschino cherries
Orange slices
1-2 cups whiskey, to taste
Decorative ice ring or large crushed ice

In a large pitcher or mixing bowl, blend orange juice, lemonade, sugar, soda, bitters, and whiskey sour mix. Pour mixture into punch bowl; add cherries and orange slices and stir in whiskey. Add ice and serve.

This may be made a day ahead of serving up to the addition of the fruit, whiskey and ice. Pour into large jars and refrigerate. Add cherries, orange slices whiskey and ice just before serving.

This recipe is easily doubled or tripled to serve a large group.

BAYOU LIBERTY PIROGUE RACES
PHOTO BY GILDA PERKINS

Maque Choux

12 ears fresh, tender corn
1/4 cup canola oil
1 large yellow onion, chopped
2 cloves garlic, minced
1 large red bell pepper, chopped
1 green bell pepper, chopped
2 small jalapenos, minced (ribs and seeds removed)
2 tablespoons chopped fresh parsley
1/2 teaspoon ground red pepper
Salt to taste

To prepare corn, shuck and clean ears well, removing silks. Cut kernels off ears twice, and then scrape cobs with the edge of a spoon before discarding cobs. Set corn aside.

Heat canola oil in a large saucepan over medium heat and sauté onion, garlic, bell peppers and jalapenos for about 5 minutes. Add reserved corn, parsley, red pepper and salt. Continue cooking for about 30 minutes, stirring often. Serve hot.

Pronounced "mock shoe", this Louisiana staple is thought to be a Cajun take on a very old Native American Dish. What a great way to use our beautiful local produce!

"WE CAN NEVER HAVE ENOUGH OF NATURE"
HENRY DAVID THOREAU, *WALDEN POND*

IT GOES LIKE THIS, DAD
PHOTO BY MARY PAT LANDRY

BAYOU LIBERTY RISING
PHOTO BY CHARLOTTE LOWRY COLLINS (PHOTO ALSO FEATURED ON THE COVER)

ALL SAINTS DAY

All Saints Day, a Roman Catholic solemnity, is celebrated on November 1st, the day after All Hallows Eve (Halloween). There are many traditions associated with All Saints Day in other countries and other parts of the United States but there is one common to the Bayou Liberty area. For days before All Saints Day, the graves of loved ones are cleaned and painted. On the night of All Saints, lighted candles and flowers fill the cemeteries as people roam from one cemetery to another, offering prayers for deceased relatives and friends.

Funerals also have special customs in the Bayou Liberty area. Following tradition, the body of the deceased is placed on a boat. The family and then friends follow in other boats "down the bayou" to the church. After the service and burial, all return to the family home for a sumptuous feast and celebration of the life of the deceased.

PHOTO BY GILDA PERKINS

Old Fashioned Bread Pudding with Rum Sauce

Bread Pudding:
3   cups soft bread cubes (4 cups for firmer pudding)
2   cups milk
4   tablespoons butter
1/2 cup sugar
2   eggs, lightly beaten
1/4 teaspoon salt
1   teaspoon cinnamon
1/2 cup raisins or chopped apple

Preheat oven to 350 degrees. Place bread cubes into a 1 1/2 quart baking dish. Scald milk and butter.

Blend remaining ingredients with milk mixture and pour into baking dish. Place dish into a larger pan with about 1 inch of hot water. Bake 40 to 45 minutes or until a knife inserted about 1 inch from the edge comes out clean. Serve warm with Rum Sauce.

Rum Sauce:
2/3 cup evaporated milk
2/3 cup water
3   tablespoons sugar
3   teaspoons cornstarch
     Pinch of salt
1   teaspoon butter
1   jigger (1 1/2 ounces) rum

Rum Sauce:
Heat milk and water in a small saucepan. Combine sugar, cornstarch and salt. Stir into the heated milk and cook until slightly thickened and smooth; add butter and cool.

Before serving, stir in rum and spoon over individual servings of the bread pudding. Brandy may be substituted for the rum, if desired.

Lemon Squares

Crust:
2   cups sifted all-purpose flour
1/2 cup confectioner's sugar
1/4 teaspoon salt
1   cup melted butter

Preheat oven to 350 degrees.

Mix flour, sugar and salt until blended. Stir in melted butter and press mixture into the bottom of a 9 x 13-inch baking dish. Bake for 20 minutes. Cool slightly.

Filling:
4   eggs, beaten
2   cups sugar
5   tablespoons fresh lemon juice
4   tablespoons all-purpose flour
1 1/2 tablespoons lemon zest
     Confectioner's sugar for dusting

Mix all ingredients well and pour over cooled crust. Bake for 25-30 minutes. Cool and dust with confectioner's sugar before cutting into squares to serve.

He leads me beside the still waters, He restores my soul. Psalm 23:2-3

Solitude III — PHOTO BY
CHARLOTTE LOWRY COLLINS

Drunken Chicken

First of all, you will need 2 metal chicken stands, the kind that will hold a can of beer. These may be purchased at almost any kitchen specialty store.

2   3-pound whole chickens
     Salt, pepper and Creole seasoning to
     taste

2   (12-ounce) cans beer

Clean chickens and season well with salt, pepper and Creole seasoning; allow them to come to room temperature, about 1 hour.

Pour out about 1/3 of the beer in each can and place them on the stands. Place chickens on the stands, legs downward.

Set stands on a heavy baking sheet with enough lip to catch drippings. Covering the sheet with foil will aid in clean-up later.

Grill at 350 degrees for about 1 1/4 hours or until internal temperature in the thigh reaches 170 degrees.

Chickens should be golden browned with

crispy skin by this time. Remove chickens from grill and cover with foil; allow to rest about 20 minutes.

Carefully remove chickens to a carving board; carve and serve on a warmed platter. These will serve 8-10 people.

WOOD CARVED
DECORATIVE MALLARD
BY KENNETH KINCADE

First you make a roux...

THEN ADD GARLIC AND THE CAJUN TRINITY: ONIONS, CELERY AND BELL PEPPER.

ONIONS AND GARLIC
OIL BY BRUCE HUME

The Blackwell Girls' Grits and Grillades

GRITS:

- cups water
- tablespoon salt
- cup grits, uncooked
- tablespoons butter
- (3-ounce) roll garlic or jalapeno processed cheese
- pound sharp Cheddar cheese, grated
- tablespoons Worcestershire sauce

Preheat oven to 350 degrees. Spray a baking dish with cooking spray and set aside.

Add water and salt to a large saucepan and bring to a boil. Slowly stir in grits and cook according to package directions.

Once they are done, stir in butter, processed cheese, Cheddar cheese and Worcestershire sauce. Stir until butter and cheeses are melted and pour mixture into prepared baking dish. Cook for 15 minutes.

Note: This freezes well and the recipe may be easily doubled for a larger group. As a main dish this recipe will serve 4-6 people.

GRILLADES:

- 2 round steaks, cut into 8 equal portions
- 2 tablespoons all-purpose flour
- Salt and pepper to taste
- 2-3 tablespoons vegetable oil for browning
- 3/4 cup vegetable oil
- 3/4 cup all-purpose flour
- 2 medium onions, coarsely chopped
- 2 (10-ounce) cans tomatoes with green chilies
- Salt and black pepper to taste

Season 2 tablespoons flour with salt and pepper to taste. Lightly flour steaks on both sides. Heat 2-3 tablespoons of vegetable oil in a large skillet and lightly brown steaks. Sear on both sides and remove to a plate.

Make roux by adding 3/4 cup vegetable oil and 3/4 cup flour in skillet. Cook, stirring constantly, until roux is dark. Add onion and sauté about 5 minutes, continuing to stir mixture. Add tomatoes and simmer for about 5 minutes. Add round steaks and cover with a tight-fitting lid. (This is a very important step!) Simmer on low for 2-3 hours. Leave lid in place and do not add additional liquid. Taste and adjust seasonings as needed before serving.

Serve grillades over the hot grits.

Seafood Gumbo

- 1/2 cup vegetable oil
- 1/2 cup all-purpose flour
- 1 cup chopped celery
- 1 cup chopped onion
- 1 large green pepper, seeded/chopped
- 1 cloves garlic, minced
- 3 pound okra, sliced
- 1 pound cooked ham, diced
- 1 quart seafood stock or chicken broth
- 1 quart water
- 1 cup Worcestershire sauce
- 1/4 bay leaf
- 1 teaspoon thyme
- 1 teaspoon red pepper flakes
- 1/2 pounds medium shrimp, peeled and deveined
- 2 pound fresh lump crabmeat
- Gumbo file, optional
- 1 Hot cooked rice

Heat oil in a large Dutch oven; add flour and cook over medium heat, stirring constantly, until roux is caramel-colored. Stir in celery, onion, green pepper and garlic and cook until onion is transparent. Add okra and ham and continue cooking for about 10 minutes. Add stock or broth, water, Worcestershire, bay leaf, thyme and red pepper flakes; bring to a boil. Reduce heat and simmer mixture for 1 hour, stirring occasionally.

Add shrimp and crabmeat to gumbo and return to heat, cooking only until shrimp are pink. Before serving, remove and discard bay leaf and stir in file, if using. Serve over rice.

This recipe makes about 12 cups of gumbo.

Cajun Seafood Boil

4 small onions
4 ribs celery
2 heads garlic
5 tablespoons salt
6 lemons, quartered
1 bag Zatarain's Crab Boil
New potatoes, washed and scrubbed
Corn-on-the-cob (ears cut in half)
5 pounds shrimp
Fresh crabs, optional

Fill a large seafood pot about two-thirds full of water. Add onions, celery, garlic, salt, lemons, and crab boil mix. Bring to a rapid boil; add potatoes and return to boil. Add corn and return to boil.

Add shrimp and boil for about 6 minutes. If using crabs, they may be added along with the shrimp.

Saucy Crawfish Pasta

1 pound rotini pasta
8 tablespoons butter, divided
6 green onions, chopped
2 cloves garlic, minced
1 tablespoons tomato paste
1/2 crawfish tails
2 pound Andouille sausage, diced
cups half-and-half
Creole seasoning to taste
1/4 cup finely chopped fresh parsley, for garnish

Cook pasta according to package directions in salted boiling water. Drain, return to pot and stir in 4 tablespoons of butter. Cover and set aside to keep warm.

In a heavy pot, melt remaining 4 tablespoons of butter. Sauté onions and garlic for 3 minutes, stirring constantly. Add tomato paste, crawfish and sausage and continue cooking for 15 minutes.

Add half-and-half and Creole seasoning and continue cooking over low heat until sauce thickens. Combine with reserved rotini and serve hot.

This makes 4-6 generous servings.

SPRINGTIME IN PARADISE
OIL BY MARY CHRISTOPHER

Two Grand Ladies of Bayou Liberty

The Bayou Liberty area was home to two women who left a profound mark on the community through their dedication and service. Both June Landry and Hatsy Roberts moved to Slidell from New Orleans.

June Landry

June was a Girl Scout leader, a member of the Slidell Women's Civic Club, and the Ozone Camellia Club, and served as a Queen of the Krewe of Slidellians. She and her husband were instrumental in raising the money necessary to air condition Slidell High School.

Cheryl Landry, speaking of her late mother: "Always in her heart and deep within her soul, was the love for her family, friends and church as well as her community."

Hatsy Robbert

Her name was Friederica Wilhelmina Emilie Robbert, but everyone called her "Hatsy." She was born and raised in New Orleans where she worked for the IRS for 31 years.

After retiring, she bought a home in the Bayou Liberty area. There she created unique baskets and hats made from long leaf pine needles. She designed pottery pieces that she fired in her own kiln and printed napkins and invitations on an old printing press. Her hands were never idle.

A member of the Slidell Garden Club, she taught her crafts to many Slidellians and was loved by everyone who knew her for her kindness and her ready smile. Hatsy died in 2000 at the age of 108.

This is a poem Hatsy wrote after the death of a dear friend:

We took a long, last ride together.

Yet alone on the train we sped.

My heart was broken,

My thoughts unspoken,

For he was in the baggage car ahead.

Bells tolled in Forest Hills Cemetery.

Beneath the sod he was laid to rest.

I just cannot see

Why he was taken from me.

Yet they say God's ways are best.

George B. Dunbar

One of Slidell's most renowned artists is George B. Dunbar, a native of New Orleans, who has lived and worked in Slidell since the 1970s.

After graduating high school, Dunbar served in the U.S. Navy before studying at the Tyler School of Art at Temple University in Philadelphia. One reason for selecting Tyler was "because of the location --- I could see art shows on the weekends in New York." After graduating in 1951, he toured Europe for a year and then returned home. He exhibited work at a gallery in New Orleans and conducted workshops at the Tulane University School of Architecture.

In the mid-50s, he and five other artists created the Orleans Gallery, an artist cooperative gallery. The New Orleans Museum of Art and the Orleans Gallery have been acknowledged as the beginning of the contemporary art scene in New Orleans.

It was then he found a second career interest: real estate development. He turned his attention to the Slidell area, developing waterfront sites which he felt were important physical and psychological elements of local traditions. His days were spent on real estate; his nights, art work.

Today his focus remains on the art he creates in his studio in Bayou Liberty.

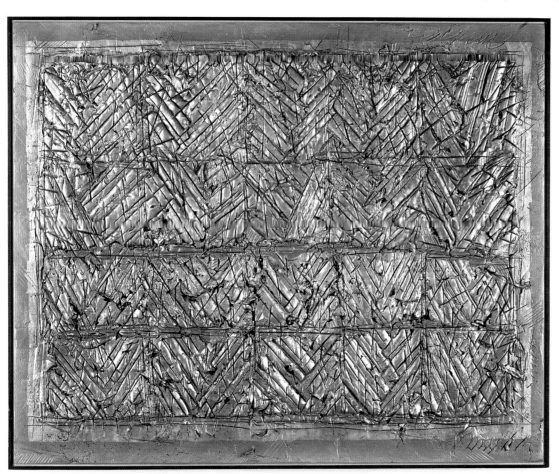

Marsh Grass
PALLADIUM LEAF OVER GREEN CLAY BY GEORGE DUNBAR

LAKE PONTCHARTRAIN

THE CAMPS AT CARR
PHOTO BY MARY PAT LANDRY

Savoring Slidell

Pontchartrain's Pride

Some Slidellians live on her banks; some make a living from her waters; and for some, it is recreation extraordinaire. For all, Lake Pontchartrain defines our boundaries; adds character to our culture, and provides a significant source of pride.

Sailing Along Lake Pontchartrain
Watercolor by Lucy Band

Lake Pontchartrain Crab Cakes

1/2 cup mayonnaise
3 tablespoons finely chopped green pepper
2 tablespoons finely chopped pimento
4 tablespoons grated onion
1 pound back fin or select crabmeat, well picked
1 teaspoon dry mustard
2 teaspoons Worcestershire sauce
Salt to taste
1/4 teaspoon cayenne pepper
1 egg, lightly beaten
1-2 sleeves saltine crackers, finely crushed
Butter

In a small bowl, mix together mayonnaise, green pepper, pimento and onion. Cover with plastic wrap and microwave for 1 or 2 minutes, until vegetables are tender.

Place crabmeat in a larger bowl and add steamed mixture to it. Add mustard, Worcestershire sauce, salt, pepper and egg. Mix ingredients very gently, with hands, to prevent breaking up crab pieces. Shape mixture into patties and dip in cracker crumbs until well coated. Place on a baking sheet and chill for 30 minutes before serving.

Melt desired amount of butter in a frying pan and cook patties over medium heat until golden brown, turning only once.

To-Die-For Crab Dip

1 (8-ounce) package cream cheese, softened
8 ounces lump crabmeat
Squeeze of fresh lemon juice
1/2 cup Creole mustard
1/2 cup mayonnaise
2 green onions, chopped

Spread softened cream cheese on a serving plate. Spread crabmeat over cream cheese and spritz with lemon juice.

In a small bowl, mix together Creole mustard and mayonnaise, stirring well to blend. Spoon mixture over crabmeat in dish and top with chopped green onions. Serve with toast points.

NOTE: The mustard/mayonnaise mixture is also delicious served with boiled shrimp.

page 100

BEAUTIFUL SWIMMER
PASTEL BY JENNIFER JOFFRION

Elegant Crabmeat Soup

4   tablespoons butter
1   medium onion, finely diced
2   cloves garlic, pressed
2   tablespoons tomato paste
1   (14.5-ounce) can chicken broth
1/2 cup water
1   (12-ounce) can evaporated milk
1   pound lump crabmeat, picked well
2   green onion tops, finely sliced, for
     garnish
     White pepper, optional

In a large, heavy saucepan over medium heat, melt butter. Sauté onion and garlic for about 3 minutes; add tomato paste and sauté another 2 minutes, stirring constantly. Stir in broth and water; reduce heat to low and simmer for about 20 minutes; add milk and stir well. Fold in crabmeat gently, taking care to avoid breaking it up.

Ladle into warm serving bowls and garnish with green onion and white pepper, if desired.

This makes 4 servings and may be easily doubled.

Northshore Harbor Center

The Conference Center for the Future

Event planners have learned that trade shows and exhibitions are among the most cost-effective marketing tools available today. With attendance at these events topping 123 million people last year, savvy planners are looking for the biggest bang for their bucks in selecting a venue to host their conferences, seminars, trade shows, social events, and other functions. Companies and organizations from throughout the region have discovered that the Northshore Harbor Center fills the bill for all their needs.

Located just minutes from New Orleans' historic French Quarter, the Northshore Harbor Center offers exceptional value and convenience. Nearby are more than 2,000 hotel rooms, two major airports, three intestate highways, a wide range of dining options, and the ambiance and charm of New Orleans and Lake Pontchartrain's North Shore.

Operated by the Northshore Harbor Center District, the Center features 45,000 square feet of quality exhibition space and meeting rooms that can accommodate groups of up to 2,500 people in a variety of settings. Patton's Catering, voted among the top five best caterers in New Orleans, provides complete food services for events at the Center.

A friendly and professionally trained staff stands ready to assist you in making your event a success at Northshore Harbor Center.

BROWN PELICAN PASTEL
BY LORETTA KINCADE

Garden Tip:
If your African violets refuse to bloom, try this: each time you
empty a milk jug, pour in a little water and use this diluted solution
to water your violets. You will not believe the blooms!

The Westchester Garden Club was founded in 1966 and its members have been active and busy ever since. Besides beautifying their own area with flowers and flag poles, their city wide efforts enabled Slidell to be named Cleanest City of the state of Louisiana. They helped co- found the Greater Slidell Council of Garden Clubs and have published two cookbooks.

Tammany Holding Company, llc

Proud Developers of Lakeshore Louisiana

On the sublime north shore of Lake Pontchartrain, in East St. Tammany Parish, a residential community like no other in the United States is taking shape. The community is rising out of 3,000 acres of Louisiana real estate in what Pierre Le Moyne d'Iberville referred to as "the most beautiful land I have yet seen" when he visited the area in 1699. That's a pretty bold statement, especially coming from an explorer who had seen quite a bit of land!

The beauty of the area that so overwhelmed d'Iberville more than four centuries ago continues to cast its spell today and is what led Bob Torres, the President and CEO of Tammany Holding Company, to select the site for his Lakeshore Louisiana development. Torres and his development team are transforming what was previously undeveloped lakefront property into a community that, when completed, will include the finest commercial and recreational amenities in support of a wide range of residential lifestyle choices for discerning homeowners. The only master-planned community on the lake's north shore, Lakeshore Louisiana is one of the largest developments of its kind in the country and is destined to become a feat of engineering and development achievements unprecedented in the state's history.

BUILDING MORE THAN HOMES

"Our goal here was to build more than a residential subdivision," Torres explains. "We wanted to create a lifestyle. Our 25-year development plan calls for Lakeshore Louisiana to eventually become a small city in itself. We're much more than just a residential community. Residents and visitors alike will enjoy the services and amenities of a full-scale waterfront, master-planned community that includes yacht harbor, professional services, dining, entertainment, and much more. Everything, in fact, that is necessary to redefine exceptional lifestyle options in Slidell and east St. Tammany Parish."

Torres and his team of professionals are well on their way to doing exactly that. Unlike many developers who acquire, develop, market, and sell residential living, Tammany Holding Company enjoys the enviable reputation of going the extra mile to create a complete lifestyle setting. Torres brought years of experience in the industry to his vision for Lakeshore Louisiana. Breaking ground in 1996, an armada of earth moving equipment dug out the deep water access that allows boaters to launch from their property into a waterway from which they can access the Gulf of Mexico and the oceans of the world. Tammany Holding Company also completed the spring water canals and Serenity Lake at Lakeshore Louisiana.

Torres' main focus was to offer a wide range of residential options that allow several generations of a family to live in the same community. Tammany Development's residential sales team sold lots in Lakeshore Louisiana to quality builders in the St. Tammany Parish area. To date, they have completed more than 200 single family homes with innovative floor plans located on lots that include gorgeous backyards, back porches, and patios. These homes are ideal for families and couples who need up to 5,000 square feet of living space. Other residential options include spacious low-rise, mid-rise, and high-rise condominiums, townhomes and garden homes, also constructed by the area's finest builders, that are perfect for empty nesters, retirees, and others seeking to downsize. The result of this careful planning and construction is that prospective homeowners can find almost anything they are looking for at Lakeshore Louisiana – whether it is smaller square footage at an affordable cost, waterfront living with a boat dock, or their own homesite on which to build the floor plan of their choice.

A COMPLETE LIFESTYLE COMMUNITY

Realizing that a community is made up of much more than homes, Torres included in the master plan for Lakeshore Louisiana the broad range of amenities that breathe life into a neighborhood.

The Boardwalk, located directly on the water, is Lakeshore Louisiana's center for retail services, shopping, dining, and entertainment. Whether homeowners and guests are looking for an evening of fine dining, a casual meal, meeting friends for a sunset cocktail, or relaxing at the local coffee shop, the restaurants at The Boardwalk offer something for every taste. In addition, residents are within a short, relaxing stroll from professional services, salons, retail stores, and small shops perfect for browsing and shopping.

The Marina at Lakeshore Louisiana is being designed to include boat slips, deep water access, and docking for sailboats, yachts, and cruisers. When completed, The Marina will also include a dry storage facility offering protection from the elements and a gasoline dock for refueling. With quick, easy access to Lake Pontchartrain, the area's deep waterways and canals are also convenient for wave runners, jet skis, canoes, kayaks, and paddle boats.

"When completed, Lakeshore Louisiana will be a lifestyle community of about 7,000 families," Torres notes. "Currently, we have about 200 single family homes and about 700 multi-family structures built and occupied. We are in close proximity to a full-service medical complex and one of the finest school systems in Louisiana. There truly is something to suit almost any taste at Lakeshore Louisiana and we look forward to showcasing what we have here to prospective homeowners."

LAKEFRONT HOME OF MR. AND MRS. ROBERT TORRES

Lishman City Market

Slidell's Neighborhood Grocer

Laura Lishman was only fourteen years old when she began working at the neighborhood grocery store that her parents, Bobby and Melanie Lishman, had opened in 1988 on Highway Eleven in Slidell. That single store has evolved into a family business that includes four full-service grocery stores encompassing almost 80,000 square feet of space showcasing the freshest fruits, vegetables, and custom-cut meats serving shoppers from throughout St. Tammany Parish. Despite the growth of their business over the years, however, the family takes great pride in retaining the atmosphere of a neighborhood grocery store where employees treat customers like family and greet them by name.

"Our customers know that a family member is working in our stores every day," explains Bobby Lishman. "Customer service was the focus of the business when we began and it remains so today. We hand cut the best and freshest cuts of meat in town. Our Pontchartrain location features one of the finest bakeries in Slidell and we prepare many quality items that can't be found in the large chain stores. We do our very best to treat each and every customer like a family member."

Bayou Street with Red Bean the Crawfish
Acrylic by Adam Sambola

(ABOVE, LEFT) *DOWN THE HATCH*
PHOTO BY LUANA KATHY PEREZ
(ABOVE) *I CAUGHT ONE*
PHOTO BY CHARLOTTE ELIAS
ANCHORAGE MARINA
PHOTO BY KIM BERGERON

Savoring Slidell

Lake Pontchartrain is renowned for its spectacular sunsets. They can be enjoyed from a boat, a backyard, or while traveling across "The Five Mile Bridge" that connects Slidell to New Orleans.

Café Au Lait Snowball

1   Double strength brewed CDM & Chicory Coffee, cold
    package Junket or similar ice cream mix, prepared as directed (not frozen)

For each drink, mix equal parts coffee and ice cream mix. Pour over crushed ice to serve.

NOTE: For those new to our area, CDM & Chicory Coffee is a regional product from Reily Foods Company. The business began as a grocery in Monroe and relocated to New Orleans in 1902 where they began to roast, grind and package coffee under the newly-created Luzianne brand.

Almond Tea

2   (1-quart) tea bags or 4 regular-size
2   cups boiling water
1 1/4   cups sugar
1/3   cup fresh lemon juice
1   teaspoon vanilla
1   teaspoon almond extract
2   cups cold water

Add tea bags to boiling water an steep for 7 minutes. Stir in all other ingredients and chill thoroughly before serving.

For a decorative presentation, freeze some of the mixture to make ice cubes and garnish with lemon slices and fresh mint.

LAKE PONTCHARTRAIN SUNSET AT TREASURE ISLE
PHOTO BY RONNIE REINE

A microplane zester, available at any kitchen store, is perfect for use with this recipe. Use it over a bowl to catch every bit of the zest. It makes it very easy to secure just the yellow zest and none of the pith.

Limoncello

1 Meyer lemons, washed & dried well
fifth quality vodka
Sugar, for simple syrup

Carefully zest lemons, making sure none of the bitter white pith is included. Place zest in a clean glass screw-top jar and add vodka. Allow mixture to sit in a cool dark place for at least 30 days.

When ready to complete, mix with equal part of simple syrup. To prepare syrup, add 2 parts of sugar to 1 part of water in a heavy sauce-pan. Bring mixture to a boil over medium heat and boil for 3 minutes, stirring constantly. Cool and add to lemon mixture; stirring to blend.

Place in freezer until ready to serve.

WONDERS OF THE SEA
OIL BY CAROL HALLOCK

Savoring Slidell

Shrimp Boats is a' Comin'...

The marine life of the lake has provided a livelihood for many people for generations. The lake is a bountiful breeding ground for oysters, crabs, shrimp and a large variety of fish. Spring spawns speckled trout; and summer, shrimp. Small brown shrimp are extremely tasty morsels that leave much of the country's palate green with envy. Locals enjoy a wide variety of culinary delights. Some of their treasured recipes are sprinkled throughout this book.

OYSTER BOAT— PHOTO BY LUANA KATHY PEREZ

Oysters Mosca

1	stick butter
1	large onion, chopped
1/2	teaspoon dried thyme
3/4	teaspoon oregano
1/3	teaspoon ground red pepper
3	cloves garlic, finely chopped
4	dozen oysters, drained and liquid reserved
	Salt and pepper to taste
1	cup seasoned breadcrumbs
2	tablespoons finely chopped parsley
	Shredded Parmesan

Preheat oven to 350 degrees.

Melt butter in a large skillet or saucepan. Stir in onion, thyme, oregano, red pepper and garlic. Cook until onion is tender and garlic is softened but not burned. Add oysters and cook until edges begin to curl; add reserved liquid. Fold in breadcrumbs and parsley.

Pour mixture into greased gratin dish or individual ramekins. Sprinkle tops with Parmesan and bake for 15-20 minutes.

Spicy Shrimp Creole

2	tablespoons canola oil
1	large onion, chopped
1	green pepper, seeded and chopped
1	red pepper, seeded and chopped
1	cup chopped celery
4	cloves garlic, pressed
2	(16-ounce) cans crushed tomatoes
2	teaspoons Creole seasoning
1/4	teaspoon salt
1/4	teaspoon cayenne pepper
1	tablespoon chopped fresh basil or 1/2 teaspoon dried
2	bay leaves
2	pounds large shrimp, peeled and deveined
	Hot cooked rice
1/2	cup chopped fresh parsley, for garnish

Add canola oil to a large, heavy pot and heat over medium. Add onion, peppers, celery and garlic and sauté for about 3 minutes or until onion is transparent, stirring constantly.

Stir in tomatoes, Creole seasoning, salt, cayenne and basil, mixing well. Add bay leaves and bring mixture to a boil. Cover and reduce heat; simmer for 30 minutes, stirring often. Add shrimp and cook for an additional 5 minutes or until shrimp turn pink. DO NOT overcook.

Remove bay leaves before serving and spoon over hot rice. Garnish with fresh parsley.

This dish serves 6 to 8 people

SHRIMP! SHRIMP! SHRIMP!

Caught in trawlers, skiffs, and lugers they are boiled, stewed, fried, stuffed, and added to gumbos, jambalyas and etoufees.

Eggplant & Shrimp Casserole

3   eggplants, peeled and cubed
2   tablespoons butter, divided
    cup chopped onion
    cup chopped celery
    green pepper, seeded and chopped
    cloves garlic, finely minced
    center-cut ham slice, minced
1   pounds shrimp, peeled and deveined
1   cup chicken broth
1/2 teaspoon Italian seasoning
    teaspoon cayenne pepper
    Salt to taste
2   sleeves saltine crackers, crushed and divided

Boil eggplant in 2 quarts of water until tender, taking care not to overcook. Drain well and set aside.

Preheat oven to 350 degrees. Lightly spray a 9 x 13-inch baking dish with cooking spray and set aside.

In a large pot, melt 4 tablespoons of butter and add onion, celery, green pepper and garlic. Sauté until vegetables are tender and onion is transparent. Stir in ham and shrimp and cook until shrimp are pink. Add eggplant, broth, seasonings and half the cracker crumbs. Stir gently to combine and spoon mixture into prepared baking dish. Cover dish with remaining cracker crumbs. Melt remaining butter and drizzle over the dish; bake for 30 minutes or until golden browned.

This casserole, as a side dish, will serve 8 people.

NOTE: Use any size shrimp that are available, but if they are very large they should be cut into more manageable bite-sized pieces.

Shrimp Pasta Salad

1   (16-ounce) bag of tri-color pasta
4   tomatoes, chopped
1   bunch green onions, chopped
1/2 cup finely chopped green pepper
1   cup chopped black olives
1   (14-ounce) can artichoke hearts, drained and diced
1   tablespoon dried thyme
1   tablespoon garlic powder
1/3 cup olive oil
1   bottle Italian salad dressing
    Salt and black pepper to taste

Cook pasta according to package directions and drain well. Add all remaining ingredients and mix well.

Cover and refrigerate overnight or several hours before serving.

Crawfish Pie

1   stick butter
1   container Creole seasoning
3   cloves garlic, chopped
1/4 cup all-purpose flour
1   (10.75-ounce) can cream of mushroom soup
1   (10.75-ounce) can cream of celery soup
1   pound crawfish tails, chopped
1   teaspoon hot sauce
1   tablespoon sherry or white wine
    Salt and pepper to taste
    Small pastry shells (16-20) or mini filo cups (30-45)

Preheat oven to 350 degrees.

In a large skillet, melt butter. Add Creole seasoning and garlic and cook until garlic is tender. Stir in flour and cook over low heat for 5 to 7 minutes, stirring constantly. Add soups and crawfish tails, hot sauce and sherry or wine. Mix well and adjust seasonings.

Place pastry shells or filo cups on large baking sheets. Fill each with crawfish mixture and bake about 10-15 minutes or until hot through.

FRESH OYSTERS
ACRYLIC ON TRAVERTINE TILE
BY LEE MCELVEEN

Big Crowd Artichoke and Oyster Soup

1 pound margarine
8 cups finely chopped green onion, bulbs and stems
1 gallon artichoke hearts, drained and quartered
2 jars instant chicken bouillon
3 quarts heavy cream
3/4 cup all-purpose flour
2 dozen medium oysters, chopped
2 quarts milk

Melt margarine in a heavy-bottom stockpot over medium heat. Add onions and sauté until transparent; add salt and pepper to taste and stir to incorporate.

Slowly add artichokes, stirring until blended, and cook for 10 minutes. Add chicken bouillon and heavy cream and continue cooking for 5 minutes. Reduce heat to low and gently stir in flour; cook for an additional 15 minutes.

Add oysters and continue cooking, stirring often and thinning with milk as needed. When ready to serve, remove desired amount and heat in a saucepan.

Note: This serves 15 to 20 people so it is a great recipe to make and divide into smaller servings. It freezes beautifully. Also, to speed preparation, oysters may be chopped in a blender or food processor; pulse often so they aren't over-processed.

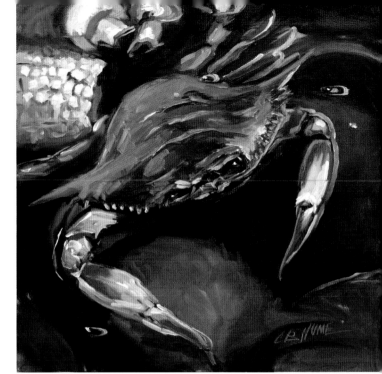

CRAB BOIL
OIL ON CANVAS BY BRUCE HUME

Oyster Patties

1/4 cup margarine
1 rounded tablespoon all-purpose flour
2 bunches green onions, finely chopped
1 (10.5-ounce) can cream of mushroom soup
4 dozen oysters, drained and chopped
Tony Chachere's Creole Seasoning, to taste
1 dozen medium-sized patty shells

Melt margarine in large frying pan. Add flour and brown lightly; stir in green onions and cook, stirring, until wilted (a few minutes). Preheat oven to 350 degrees.

Add soup and chopped oysters to frying pan. Add Creole seasoning as desired. Simmer mixture for 20 minutes, stirring occasionally. Cool slightly.

Place patty shells on an ungreased baking sheet and spoon cooled oyster mixture into them. Bake for about 10 minutes or until shells are crisp and lightly browned. Serve immediately.

If Tony Chachere's Creole Seasoning blend is not available, salt and pepper may be substituted. However, for best results in this dish and for many others, this Opelousas-produced seasoning is worth finding!

Chicken of the Gulf

1 (10.5-ounce) can chicken broth
2 cups seasoned breadcrumbs or corn-bread crumbs
1 cup chopped, cooked shrimp
8 ounces lump crabmeat
8 boneless chicken breasts, flattened
Salt and pepper to taste
1 cup all-purpose flour
4 eggs, beaten
1 cup milk
1 1/2 cups butter

Preheat oven to 350 degrees.

Pour enough broth over crumbs to moisten. Combine moistened crumbs with shrimp and crabmeat.

Spoon crumb mixture into the center of each chicken breast. Roll chicken up, tucking ends inside and secure with toothpicks. Mix salt and pepper with flour. Dip rolls in beaten eggs, then flour, then milk and finally in flour again.

Melt butter in a heavy skillet. When butter is bubbling, gently brown the chicken rolls. Drain on paper towels then place on a greased baking sheet to finish in the oven, about 20-25 minutes.

BANKS OF PONTCHARTRAIN

By Nancy Griffith

Well I'm back where my garden blooms all year

Where the wintertime speaks softly in the fallin' rain

And I'm goin' back to my green eyed lover there

We will dance along the banks of old Lake Pontchartrain

Coffee Punch

4 quarts very strong coffee
5 tablespoons sugar
2 quarts vanilla ice cream
5 teaspoons vanilla
1 large carton frozen whipped topping, softened

Add sugar to coffee; mix until sugar is dissolved and chill thoroughly.

When ready to serve, add ice cream to a large punch bowl. Pour chilled coffee over ice cream.

Stir vanilla into whipped topping until well-blended; fold into coffee mixture in bowl just before serving.

VIEW FROM THE BACKYARD
PHOTO BY MARY PAT LANDRY

Trout Amandine

1	cup milk
6	speckled trout fillets
1	cup all-purpose flour
1/4	teaspoon salt
8	teaspoon black pepper
1/2	tablespoons butter
	cup sliced almonds
	Juice of 1 lemon

Fishing camps along the water's edge welcome family and friends to come and sit on the pier, smell the salty air, feel the never ending breeze, and taste an icy cold beer with spicy boiled crabs. This fishing club landmark was destroyed by Hurricane Katrina, but her ghost remains and many claim to hear laughter as they exit the Five Mile Bridge on their way home from New Orleans.

Pour milk into a shallow bowl and dip each fillet. Season flour with salt and pepper; mix well. Roll each fillet in flour mixture until well coated.

Melt butter in a heavy skillet and cook fish, in batches, browning evenly on both sides. As fish is done, remove each piece to a warmed platter and set aside.

In the same skillet, add almonds to drippings and sauté over medium heat until light brown in color. Stir in lemon juice, mix well and spoon almond mixture generously over each fillet before serving.

PRESERVATION AND RESTORATION

For more than 20 years, conservationists have made Herculean efforts to restore and preserve our natural resources. Thanks to the ongoing efforts of many, including the Lake Pontchartrain Basin Foundation, shell dredging in the lake has been discontinued and the quality of the water has been restored to safe, swimmable levels. This water, much loved and enjoyed, should not be taken for granted. It must be nurtured so that generations to come will continue to live on, boat on and thrive from its bounty and refreshing waters.

(LEFT) *BP Escapee*
PASTEL BY JEAN FRONDORF

(BELOW) *Fowl Play*
PHOTO BY CAMELLA M. DIMITRI

(FOLLOWING PAGE)
The Painter's Island
OIL ON CANVAS BY PEGGY HESSE

THE WEST PEARL

ALONG THE WEST PEARL
OIL ON CANVAS
BY NOLAN J. LEFORT

Entering the West Pearl

People from all over the world come to the West Pearl River for a glimpse of a 10-foot alligator or a bald eagle soaring freely against the clear blue sky. The density of the trees, the fauna, the thick moss hanging from the trees, plus the sounds of frogs, gators, birds, and other varieties of wildlife, lend a mysterious, dark, and yet exciting feel to this part of Slidell.

Fishing camps along the river are filled with weekenders and full-time residents. Many have chosen to live in beautiful homes on the bayous and rivers that meander through the area; others create a more rustic atmosphere with traditional "camps."

Climb aboard a skiff; turn on a small outboard motor, and travel through the West Pearl with its abundance of wildlife and Southern homes with lush gardens where outdoor cooking is "King."

PHOTO BY LANA KILLEEN

(LEFT) BLENDING IN
PHOTO BY TRENTIS WHITE
(BELOW) *TROPICAL PARADISE*
WATERCOLOR BY LUCY BAND

Cajun Encounters

Bringing Louisiana to Life

It is not surprising that celebrities such as film stars Brad Pitt and Angelina Jolie, TV host Kelly Ripa, R & B king Usher, Academy Award winner Forest Whitaker, singers John Fogerty and Tommy Lee, and a host of others have selected Cajun Encounters to give them and their families the best possible touring experience in the Pelican State. For more than a decade, Cajun Encounters has been showcasing the wonders of New Orleans, the area's enchanting Swamp Country, and Louisiana's Plantation Country to people who come away with a heightened appreciation for the history, culture, and unsurpassed natural beauty that abounds in and around the Crescent City.

Owned and operated by New Orleans natives, Cajun Encounters focuses on an authentic experience. Experienced guides,

each with a passion for sharing their home with others, bring to life the history of one of America's great cities and its environs.

New Orleans City Tours—Cajun Encounters begins its city tours at the birthplace of New Orleans – the French Quarter. Experienced guides point out the Quarter's best known and most loved sights, including Jackson Square, St. Louis Cathedral, and the timeless elegance of the wrought iron balconies that grace buildings that were home to writers, artists, soldiers, and pirates.

Leaving the French Quarter, the tour includes a visit to St. Louis Cemetery and to City Park where gentlemen once settled their arguments with pistols under its Dueling Oaks. Guests can also step back in time with a look at the Garden District, the old "American Sector" of the city during its infancy.

Swamp Tour—Cajun Encounters' Swamp Tour is like no other adventure in the natural world. Expert guides present visitors with an authentic, eyeball-to-eyeball encounter with wildlife ranging from alligators, wild boar, and owls, to bald eagles, snakes, and black bears.

In addition, the Swamp Tour features a visit to an authentic Cajun village accessible only by boat. This offers a fascinating look at the culture and traditions of the French Acadian people who settled in Louisiana after their expulsion from Canada by the British.

Plantation Tours—The Plantation Tours operated by Cajun Encounters feature a journey along the Great River Road to visit Oak Alley and Laura Plantation and see what life was like for the plantation aristocracy of the antebellum period.

Oak Alley, with its quarter-mile tunnel of 28 live-oak trees that frame the great house of the plantation, was built in 1839 and reflects the elegance and luxury that defined this bygone era. A visit to Laura Plantation brings to life the fascinating stories of the four women who ran the 200-year old Creole landmark, with its "Big House" and the slave quarters.

Whether their interests lie in history, culture, or the natural world, visitors who choose Cajun Encounters to experience all that New Orleans has to offer come away with a rewarding look at the very best that the Crescent City has to offer. Tours run daily, just call 1-866-92-TOURS, or visit us at www.CajunEncounters.com.

Snippet from the Past

FRIDAY PORTER

Friday Porter was the son of a wealthy plantation owner and his mother, a slave in South Carolina. His father owned a considerable tract of land near Indian Village Road east of Slidell. He gave Friday a parcel of land and his freedom if he would come to Louisiana. Friday arrived about 1830.

Soon, Friday fell in love with Anna, a free native American/African American woman who lived in Pearlington, Mississippi. Friday's only means of transportation to visit Anna was by a crude boat that he paddled down Mill Bayou, over to East Pearl and up to Pearlington.

Because this was a long and tiring journey, Friday dug a ditch through the swamp to shorten his journey. It must have been difficult with the snakes, alligators, insects and stubborn cypress knees, but he did it. Today, it is still referred to as Friday Porter's ditch.

Eventually he married Anna and as a result, we have the Porter family who are his proud descendants.

— BY JOHN CASE.

Hot Sausage

3 pounds fresh hot sausage in casings (do not use smoked sausage)
3 large onions, cut into strips
3 green peppers, seeded and cut into strips
2 (28-ounce) cans whole, peeled tomatoes
1 (8-ounce) can tomato sauce
Salt to taste

Add sausage to a large pot, cover with water and boil for about 30 minutes. Pierce sausage with a fork every 5 minutes or so, enabling as much grease as possible to be rendered.

Drain sausage and wipe down pot. Return sausage to the pot and add all other ingredients. Bring to a boil and then reduce heat, cover and cook for about 1 hour or until vegetables are tender. Serve on hot French bread.

NOTE: This freezes well so don't be afraid to make a big batch at one time. Also, Italian sausage may be used if you like the flavor of anise and fennel.

PHOTO BY TRENTIS WHITE

OCHSNER MEDICAL CENTER – NORTH SHORE

A CONTINUUM OF CARE

JAMES NEWCOMB, M.D. AND POLLY DAVENPORT, CEO

Dr. Alton Ochsner was attending a medical meeting in Ogden, Utah in March of 1941 when he received a telegram that changed his life and, ultimately, the face of medical care in southern Louisiana. Dr. Ochsner was informed by his partners, medical school professors Drs. Edgar Burns, Guy A. Caldwell, Francis LeJeune, and Curtis Tyrone, that the $4,300 of their own money that each had contributed would establish the first private group practice clinic in New Orleans based on the models of the Mayo and the Cleveland Clinics.

That small clinic has evolved today into the Ochsner Health System, a non-profit, academic, multi-specialty healthcare system serving communities in southeast Louisiana and patients from across the United States and around the world. Ochsner is now recognized as a national leader in medical research and is one of the largest non-university based physician training centers in the nation. The mission of the founders – to put the needs of all patients first and provide a continuum of the highest quality of medical care – remains at the heart of Ochsner today.

That commitment to patient care, education, and research is at the heart of a unique coordinated neighborhood-based system that led to the founding of eight hospitals and more than 35 healthcare centers in southeast Louisiana. Ochsner Medical Center - North Shore, which had begun offering quality care in a setting conveniently located to serve patients on the north shore of Lake Pontchartrain in 1985, became part of the Ochsner family in 2010. Patients from as far away as the Mississippi Gulf Coast now travel to Ochsner North Shore to receive quality healthcare.

HEALTHCARE WITH PEACE OF MIND

Ochsner Medical Center – North Shore operates as a 165-bed acute care hospital located on the lake's north shore at Slidell. Accredited by The Joint Commission, the nation's oldest and largest hospital accreditation agency, the facility is a full-service hospital that includes a 24-hour emergency room and the only Pediatric Intensive Care Unit (PICU) on the north shore.

Ochsner Medical Center – North Shore offers peace of mind to patients and their families through the provision of numerous specialties of care:

Primary Care. Ochsner provides patients with a network of internal and family medicine physicians and pediatricians to meet the primary care needs of patients in a conveniently located neighborhood medical facility with hours to accommodate busy work and family schedules.

Pediatric Intensive Care. In addition to providing the only Pediatric Intensive Care Unit on the north shore, Ochsner pediatrics specializes in comprehensive care for the whole child – from preventive services, such as immunizations, to lifesaving care and treatments.

Neonatal Intensive Care. Physicians and nurses, specially trained in neonatal intensive care, provide intensive care services to newborns.

Cardiac Care. A team of specially trained physicians and healthcare providers, coupled with the latest technology available, work to develop breakthrough approaches to the diagnosis and treatment of cardiovascular disease.

In addition, Ochsner Medical Center – North Shore specializes in the treatment of **Sleep Disorders** and **Physical Therapy** and **Inpatient Rehabilitation Services**.

"Innovation and dedication to excellence remain our hallmarks," states Polly Davenport, RN, FACHE, the hospital's Chief Executive Officer. "Our dedicated team of more than 600 healthcare professionals takes great pride in delivering exceptional clinical care while addressing the emotional, spiritual, and practical support needs of our patients and their families. We never lose sight of the individual who is our patient. Their concerns are our concerns and their continued good health is how we measure our success."

Working closely with Davenport is James Newcomb, MD, the Vice-President of Medical Affairs. Overseeing all Ochsner North Shore services is Scott Boudreaux, the Ochsner North Shore Region CEO. Joining Boudreaux in North Shore clinic operations is Edward Martin, Jr. MD, the Regional Medical Director for the North Shore.

EXCELLENCE RECOGNIZED

The work of senior management, physicians, nurse clinicians, and ancillary staff clinicians at Ochsner Medical Center – North Shore has led to recognition on a number of national and regional stages. The hospital received the 2010 "Get With the Guidelines" Gold Performance Achievement Award from the American Heart Association. In addition, Ochsner North Shore was recognized by EQ Health Solutions with that organization's Silver Level Award for Significant Achievement, Surgical Care Improvement Project in 2008 – 2010. EQ Health Solutions also awarded Ochsner North Shore its 2010 Louisiana Hospital **CAPSTONE QUALITY AWARD**.

More recently, Ochsner Medical Center – North Shore in September 2011 was named one of the nation's top performers on key quality measures by The Joint Commission. The hospital, one of only 405 U.S. hospitals and critical access hospitals to be named to the list, earned the distinction for attaining and sustaining excellence in accountability measure data about evidence-based clinical processes that are shown to improve care for certain conditions, including heart attack, heart failure, pneumonia, and surgical care.

"This recognition is based on actual objective quality measures and is a direct result of our strategy and daily execution by our clinical team," Davenport notes. "We are blessed to be in a field such as healthcare where we make a difference in the lives of people every day. We see that difference throughout the community whether it's someone who has trusted us to provide them compassionate care or a local organization that we've partnered with for a community event."

Those partnerships have been many. Ochsner Medical Center – North Shore has been a sponsor of Jazz on the Bayou benefitting the Easter Seal Society. Other recipients of the hospital's philanthropic efforts and those of its staff members include the American Heart Association, Cystic Fibrosis, the Children's Wish Endowment, Hospice Foundation South, and other civic and charitable organizations.

Savoring Slidell

BACKYARD LIVING AT ITS BEST

The homes in the West Pearl Area are renowned for parties and gracious Southern living. The Taylor home on beautiful Doubloon Bayou has been the scene of intimate backyard barbecues as well as elegant Symphony Salon concerts.

GOLDEN SPLENDOR
PASTEL BY JENNIFER JOFFRION

PHOTO BY KAY TAYLOR

Mike Pike, a native of this area, lives on the Pearl River. Lush gardens, a tree house, as tall as the trees, overlook the swamp and river. The fragrant smell of jasmine and Mike's talents at the barbeque pit, make his home his paradise.

Marinated Pork Tenderloin

1/2	cup peanut oil
1/3	cup soy sauce
1/4	cup red wine vinegar
2	tablespoons lemon juice
3	tablespoons Worcestershire sauce
2	teaspoons garlic powder
1	tablespoon dried parsley
1	teaspoon black pepper
2	(1-pound) pork tenderloins

Mix all ingredients except the tenderloins in a large plastic zip top bag. Add tenderloins, seal bag and marinate for about 4 hours. Remove tenderloins from bag and discard marinade.

Grill tenderloins uncovered over medium heat (about 325 degrees) for 15-18 minutes or until meat thermometer reaches about 150 degrees. Remove from heat, tent with foil and allow meat to rest for at least 10 minutes before slicing to serve.

(ABOVE) PHOTO BY LUCY BAND
(RIGHT) PHOTO BY MIKE PIKE

FISH FRY FESTIVITIES

Pat and Carol Neff are the area's "Fish Fry Experts." They host casual get-togethers frying for the Rotary, Perseus (carnival organization) and the Slidell Garden Club at their fishing camp, with its impressive camellias and view of the river.

Crispy Fried Catfish

2 cups self-rising cornmeal
1 tablespoon garlic powder
1 tablespoon dried thyme, finely chopped
1 tablespoon salt
2 teaspoons black pepper
1/2 teaspoon ground red pepper
1 cup buttermilk
6 (8-ounce) catfish fillets
Cooking oil for frying (vegetable or peanut)

In a shallow baking dish, mix together cornmeal, garlic powder and thyme. In a separate small bowl, blend salt and black and red peppers.

Pour buttermilk in a shallow dish and dip a fillet in it; allow excess to drip off. Sprinkle it with the salt and pepper blend and then roll in cornmeal mixture. Repeat until all fish is coated.

Pour oil to a depth of 2 inches in a deep skillet or Dutch oven and heat to 365 degrees. Fry fillets, 2 at a time, for 3 to 4 minutes on each side. Drain well on paper towels and serve immediately.

PAT AND CAROL NEFF
PHOTO BY CHARLOTTE ELIAS

Hush Puppies

1 1/2 cups yellow cornmeal
3/4 cup all-purpose flour
4 teaspoons baking powder
3/4 teaspoon salt
2 eggs
3/4 cup milk
2 tablespoons vegetable oil
Additional oil for frying

Sift dry ingredients together and set aside. In a medium mixing bowl beat eggs; add milk and 2 tablespoons oil. Stir to blend. Slowly beat in sifted ingredients. Allow mixture to stand for 15 minutes.

Meanwhile, heat additional oil in a deep skillet. When oil is hot, drop mixture by spoonful into skillet and fry until brown.

Tartar Sauce

2/3 cup mayonnaise
1 tablespoon sweet pickle relish
1 tablespoon fresh minced parsley
1 tablespoon capers, drained and rinsed
2 tablespoons grated onion
2 tablespoons fresh lemon juice
Dash of Louisiana Hot Sauce

Mix all ingredients and stir well.

This recipe makes about 1 cup of sauce. Serve it with crispy baked or ed fish.

Cocktail Sauce

2/3 cup commercial chili sauce
1/3 cup ketchup
1/4 cup fresh lemon juice
3 tablespoons horseradish
2 teaspoons Worcestershire sauce
1/4 teaspoon Louisiana Hot Sauce

Mix all ingredients well and chill.

Super Grouper

1/2 cup butter, melted
2 tablespoons lemon juice
1/4 teaspoon garlic salt
1/2 teaspoon dried parsley
1/4 teaspoon paprika, divided
1/4 teaspoon ground white pepper
2 pounds grouper fillets
2 tablespoons mayonnaise

Preheat oven to 350 degrees.

Cover a broiler pan with aluminum foil and set aside. Combine melted butter and lemon juice in a small bowl. Brush about 2 tablespoons of mixture on foil covering broiler pan.

Mix together garlic salt, parsley, 1/8 teaspoon paprika and white pepper. Sprinkle spice mixture on both sides of fillets and place them on broiler pan.

Broil fillets until meat flakes easily with a fork, about 10 minutes. Brush fillets with remaining lemon butter and then spread lightly with mayonnaise. Sprinkle fillets with remaining paprika before serving.

"Those who dwell among the beauties and mysteries of the earth are never alone or weary of life."

—Rachel Carson

Many people have chosen to live in the West Pearl area because of its natural beauty and have designed their homes to fit in with the natural surroundings. The Henderson home, nestled among tall cypress and oaks, boasts many varieties of daylilies, irises, and other plants native to Louisiana.

BROWN HERON
PHOTO BY TRENTIS WHITE

THE HENDERSON HOME
PHOTO BY NAOMI E. SCHMIDT
COURTESY OF CATHY HENDERSON

Baby Back Ribs

1/3   cup kosher salt
1/3   cup brown sugar
2   tablespoons paprika
1   tablespoon dried thyme
1   teaspoon cayenne pepper
5   teaspoon black pepper
    pounds baby back ribs (about 4 slabs)

In a small bowl, combine all ingredients except ribs. Trim ribs as needed, being sure to remove the silver skin from the backside of the ribs. The rub will penetrate better and the ribs won't curl as much during cooking time.

Sprinkle rub heavily on all sides of the meat and massage it in well with fingers. Allow ribs to stand at room temperature for 2 hours or lightly covered in the refrigerator overnight before cooking.

Preheat oven to 350 degrees. Place ribs on a large baking pan and cover tightly with aluminum foil. Roast in oven for about 3 hours; ribs should be tender at this point.

Transfer ribs from baking pan to a medium-heat grill to finish and allow crisping. This process should take about 30 minutes and racks should be turned only one time. Watch them closely.

Cut ribs into 3 or 4-bone pieces to serve alongside your favorite commercial or homemade bar-b-que sauce.

Crunchy Cole Slaw with Sliced Almonds

6   cups finely shredded cabbage
1/2   cup sliced almonds, toasted
1 1/2   cups dried cranberries
1/2   cup diced celery
1/4   cup chopped green onion, both green and white parts
1/2   cup chopped green bell pepper

Dressing
1/2   cup mayonnaise
1 1/2   tablespoons sweet pickle relish
1 1/2   tablespoons honey mustard
1 1/2   tablespoons honey
    Salt and black pepper to taste

In a large mixing bowl with a lid, combine all ingredients for slaw. Cover and refrigerate until ready to serve.

To prepare dressing, add all ingredients to a glass jar with a tight fitting lid. Shake well to blend and refrigerate. Just before serving, add dressing to slaw ingredients and mix well.

The combination of sweet and tart, along with its crunchy texture, makes this the perfect side dish for any number of foods. You won't be disappointed.

PHOTO BY CHARLETTE T. HAYES

Deep South, Deep-Fried Gator

1 bottle Italian salad dressing
Tony Chachere's Cajun Seasoning, divided
Louisiana hot sauce, to taste
4-5 pounds alligator meat, cut into 2 x 3-inch cubes
2 cups Italian-seasoned breadcrumbs
2 cups all-purpose flour
Oil, for cooking (canola, vegetable or peanut)

In a large capacity zip top plastic bag, mix Italian dressing with Tony Chachere's and hot sauce to taste. Add alligator cubes and squeeze bag to cover meat with marinade. Set bag in a large baking dish and refrigerate for two days before cooking.

When ready to prepare, mix breadcrumbs and flour in a shallow dish, adding Cajun seasoning as desired; mix well. Drain meat of excessive marinade and dredge in breadcrumb mixture.

Heat about 4 inches of oil in a heavy pot. When desired temperature is reached, deep fry the alligator in the hot oil until golden browned. Drain on paper towels on a rack before serving.

Savoring Slidell

"It's difficult to think anything but pleasant thoughts while eating a home grown tomato."

LEWIS GRIZZARD

Vegetable gardens have long been a source of joy and pride for Slidellians. Cultivating the soil, watching colorful fruits and vegetables sprout and grow, harvesting its bounty (to eat and share with neighbors and friends) is an essential part of a Slidell summer.

Green Bean and Artichoke Augratin

1/2 cup olive oil
3 cloves garlic, minced
2 bunches green onions, chopped
3 (14.5-ounce) cans French style green beans, drained and rinsed
2 (8.5-ounce) cans artichoke hearts, chopped
Black pepper to taste
1/2 cup shredded Parmesan
1 cup seasoned fine dry breadcrumbs
1 small can French-fried onions

Preheat oven to 350 degrees.

Add olive oil to a large skillet and briefly sauté garlic. Stir in beans and artichokes and sauté about 2 minutes. Add black pepper to taste. Remove from heat and stir in Parmesan and breadcrumbs. Spoon mixture into a lightly greased casserole dish.

Sprinkle French-fried onions over top of dish and bake about 25 minutes or until hot through.

Squash Casserole

8 tablespoons butter
1/2 medium onion, chopped
1/2 rib celery, chopped
1/2 green pepper, seeded and chopped
1 pound sliced or cubed yellow squash, partially cooked
2 tablespoons mayonnaise
1 tablespoon sugar
1/2 cup chopped water chestnuts
1 egg, lightly beaten
Grated cheddar cheese
1 sleeve round buttery crackers, crushed
Freshly grated Parmesan

Preheat oven to 350 degrees. Spray a casserole dish or gratin pan with cooking spray and set aside.

In a large saucepan, melt butter and sauté onion, celery and pepper until tender. Add squash to mixture.

Stir in mayonnaise and sugar; add water chestnuts. Stir and simmer a few minutes until squash is tender. Cool slightly and add egg, mixing well.

Pour mixture into prepared dish and sprinkle grated Cheddar cheese over the top. Cover that with a layer of the cracker crumbs and finish with a sprinkling of Parmesan. Bake uncovered for 30 minutes.

PICTURED ARE ISABELLE, REN AND DYLAN, GRANDCHILDREN OF ED AND GWEN LEININGER

Indian Village

Indian Village, known to many as "The Village" is an unincorporated area off Highway 190 E, known to many as Shortcut Road. Deeply rooted in the Methodist Church, the families of Indian Village were devastated when their church was burned by an arsonist in 1965. The church, Hartzell Mt. Zion United Methodist Church, was destroyed once again, in 2005 by Hurricane Katrina. Once again, it was rebuilt, this time with the addition of a Family Life Center.

Dora Jackson writes about growing up in Indian Village, remembering a happy childhood. "We didn't know we were poor." The Village had three Mom and Pop grocery stores, opened by Sam Porter, Augustine Crawford and Calvin Harrison. At times there was only one telephone available to the entire community --- good news, bad news, births, death --- all reported on that one phone.

Entertainment for the whole family was planned for Saturday nights with fish fries, chicken stew, potato salad, gumbo and homemade ice cream. "Everyone had a garden, chickens, a few pigs and maybe a milk cow."

John D. Alfred's schooner helped connect the Village with Pearlington, Mississippi. Elijah Alfred was the first commercial fisherman. Willie Hyde rented boats and was a fishing guide. Some of the other families whose roots are in the Indian Village include Smith, Prevost, Jackson, Collins, Brookter, Square, Wesley, Cade, Fields and Vaultz, to name a few.

PHOTO OF DORA ALFRED JACKSON AND FAMILY

Eggplant Fritters

1 large eggplant, peeled and diced
2 teaspoons finely chopped onion
1 egg, lightly beaten
1/3 cup all-purpose flour
2 teaspoons baking powder
1/2 teaspoon salt
3/4 teaspoon black pepper
Vegetable oil for frying

Boil eggplant until tender; drain well. Mash eggplant to yield 1 cup of pulp. Add remaining ingredients, except oil, and mix well.

Heat a small amount of vegetable oil in a large skillet. Drop eggplant mixture by spoonful into hot oil. Cook until lightly browned, turning once to brown both sides.

Turtle Soup

3	pounds turtle meat
1 1/2	pounds boneless beef cubes
5	tablespoons oil, divided
3	tablespoons all-purpose flour
3	large onions, chopped
6	cloves garlic, minced
2	green peppers, seeded and diced
4	(14.5-ounce) cans crushed tomatoes
1	(6-ounce) can tomato paste
2	ribs celery, diced
1	bunch green onions, chopped
4	bay leaves
8	whole cloves
8	whole allspice
1	lemon, sliced
	Salt and black pepper to taste
	Tony Chachare's Seasoning to taste
6	hard-cooked eggs, peeled and coarsely chopped
	Sherry to taste

Pat meat dry; add 2 tablespoons of oil or margarine to a skillet and heat. Lightly brown meat and transfer to a large Dutch oven. Cover with water and bring to a boil; lower heat to simmer and cover pot.

Meanwhile, wipe down skillet and add remaining 3 tablespoons of oil or margarine and the flour. Cook flour to make a medium-colored roux. Add chopped onion, garlic, green pepper, tomatoes and tomato paste. Cook over low heat for 45 minutes, stirring often.

Add roux mixture to browned meat, along with enough hot water to make soup. Stir in celery, green onion, bay leaves, cloves, allspice, lemon slices and seasonings. Cover and cook until meat is tender, about 2 to 3 hours.

To serve, mash chopped egg with the back of a fork. Ladle soup into warmed bowls and sprinkle with egg; stir in sherry to taste.

A love of the wild, natural beauty of the area has attracted artists and artisans. Sonny Miller, a renowned taxidermist keeps our wildlife beautiful forever. Here he shares his talent with school children.

TURTLE LOVE
PHOTO BY LUANA KATHY PEREZ

PHOTO BY GILDA PERKINS

VERRET ROYALTY
OIL BY MICKEY ASCHE

Snippet from the Past

ARTHUR JONES

Arthur Jones was a unique character that arrived in Slidell in the late 1950s. He loved animals, both to rescue and kill. He said he killed 632 elephants and 63 men and that he regretted the elephants more. He established a small zoo next to the White Kitchen in the West Pearl area. He was also a mercenary and airplane enthusiast. He would land his airplanes on Highway 90 and park them beside the road. He also had a television show called Wild Cargo.

Although Arthur came from an educated family, he did not finish high school. In the late 1960s, he invented an exercise machine. It was a success and he named it Nautilus, which became the best known name in exercise equipment. With his wealth he moved to Florida and built a large wild game refuge with facilities to land any size aircraft including his own Boeing 727. He married six times, the youngest wife being sixteen and the oldest twenty. Since his death, part of his refuge has become an exclusive fly-in residential development where owners can park their planes, regardless of size, in their driveway. It is called Jumbolair and is the home of John Travolta and others.

—BY JOHN CASE

"Working with clay is an escape for me. I am able to travel away from the worries and chaos that surround us, and enter into a world of creative splendor. I love getting lost in the simple pleasure of making things with my own hands. I strive for my work to represent the beauty that is in the frailties and imperfections of life. Working with clay reminds me of how God, like the potter, sculpts us into things of beauty that we are not able to become on our own,"

—KELLY LANDRUM-HAMMELL

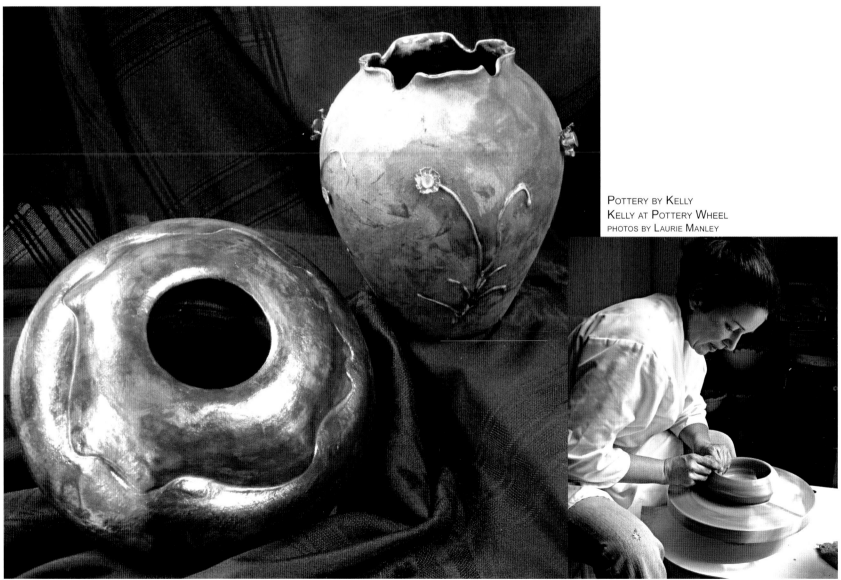

POTTERY BY KELLY
KELLY AT POTTERY WHEEL
PHOTOS BY LAURIE MANLEY

The Magnolia Forest Garden Club was organized in 1979 and federated in 1980. The club is renowned for the awards they have won for flowering arranging. They received "Best in Show" for the prestigious "Art in Bloom" in New Orleans, and were featured in a national magazine.

MAGNOLIA
OIL BY PHIL GALATAS

Garden Tip:

The West Pearl area has soil and climate for growing delicious citrus fruit. The Meyer lemon is a large lemon with a mild flavor harvested in the late fall and winter. The juice can be frozen and used year round for delicious drinks and desserts.

The Front Porch Swing

By Richard Netherland Cook

Sitting in the front porch swing,
With a cool wind in your face,
Can cause one to dream.
Of another time and place.
Back when times were simple,
Times you cannot replace,
Life was easy going then,
People moved a slower pace.
Swinging in the old porch swing,
Troubles seemed to fade,
And the problems of the day,
Could somehow be delayed.
The perfect place to sit and talk,
And to wile away the hours,
To breathe in all the country air,
And smell the garden flowers.

Sitting in the swing at twilight,
As darkness comes along,
Watching all the lightning bugs,
Listening to the cricket's song.
Maybe your dear Grandma,
Sat in the swing with you,
And told you many stories,
Of all the things she knew.
There was always lots of gossip,
Coming from the old porch swing,
When neighbors got together,
You might hear most anything.
When I think of the old porch swing,
And all it does impart,
It leaves me with fond memories
And a warm place in my heart.

OIL BY LINDA DUCOTE
COURTESY OF KATHRYN B. JONES

Meyer Lemon Ice Box Delight

First layer:
1 1/2 cups all-purpose flour
1 cup finely chopped pecans
1 1/2 sticks butter, melted

Preheat oven to 325 degrees.

Mix flour and pecans until well-blended. Pour in melted butter and stir to incorporate. Press mixture into the bottom of a 9 x 13-inch glass baking dish. Bake crust for 20 minutes and allow to cool.

Second layer:
11 ounces cream cheese, softened
1 3/4 cups confectioner's sugar
1 (8-ounce) container frozen whipped topping, thawed

With an electric mixer, blend cream cheese and sugar until blended and smooth. Fold in whipped topping and spoon mixture over the cooled crust.

Third layer:
2 eggs, lightly beaten
7/8 cup Myer lemon juice
2 (14-ounce) cans sweetened condensed milk

Blend eggs and lemon juice well. Mix in condensed milk until mixture is smooth. Spread over second layer.

Fourth layer:
2 cups heavy cream
1/3 cup sugar

Whip heavy cream with mixer on high until thickened. Gradually add sugar and whip until fluffy. Spoon over the third layer using the back of a spoon to create peaks.

Cover with plastic wrap and refrigerate several hours before serving.

Note: This contributor says she likes to make this the day before serving to be sure it is thoroughly chilled. She also noted that it freezes very well; simply allow to thaw a bit in the refrigerator before serving time.

LARGER THAN LIFE

Johnny Smith—businessman, entrepreneur, developer, and philanthropist--- started his first business while still in high school, purchasing two dump trucks for "no money down." A fearless risk-taker, he soon turned his minimal investment into a vast empire.

He and his wife, Jan, came to Slidell in the late 1970s. They amassed a small fortune by developing many of Slidell's early subdivisions, investing in real estate and providing hurricane cleanup locally and internationally.

Johnny lived a fast-paced, colorful life, which tragically ended as the result of heart failure at the age of 56. Although he was well known for his business ventures, he supported many local worthy causes, including K-Bar-B Youth Ranch, Rainbow Child Care Center, and East St. Tammany Mental Health Association.

He was the "idea man;" Jan was the self-described "details person." Many charity events were staged at their fabulous home on the Rigolets. Johnny accidentally stumbled upon the property in 1988 while rabbit hunting. He built their modern mansion near the foot of the Rigolets Bridge. Due to its unique architecture and ideal location, the house has been featured in several movies, TV commercials, and music videos.

In 2002, Jan remarried. She, and her husband, Quentin Stumpf, endured the devastation of Hurricane Katrina and painstakingly recreated the entertainment showplace to its original splendor.

With its majestic sunrises, breathtaking sunsets, and spectacular views of the lakes, the home provides a unique window into Slidell's natural beauty. Fishing boats glide past, brown pelicans soar overhead, and egrets fish on the shoreline.

PHOTO BY JOHN MONTELEPRE
COURTESY OF JAN SMITH STUMPF

Savoring Slidell

LEAVING THE WEST PEARL

As you leave the West Pearl, travel via car down Apple Pie Ridge Road onto Highway 90 to the Rigoletes, and visit historic Fort Pike built in 1880. The bridge at the Rigoletes joins St. Tammany and Orleans Parishes, and residents on both sides enjoy the site for picnicking, fishing and a stroll through history.

APPLE PIE RIDGE ROAD
PHOTO BY WANDA REISS JENSON
COURTESY OF KATHRYN B. JONES

RECIPE INDEX

Almond Tea	108
Artichoke Yummies	52
Baby Back Ribs	131
Best Milk Punch Ever	42
Big Crowd Artichoke and Oyster Soup	113
Cajun Seafood Boil	94
Cheesy Shrimp On Grits Toast	53
Chicken of the Gulf	113
Coconut Pound Cake	27
Coffee Punch	114
Colorful Cucumber Stacks	70
Corn & Crawfish Soup	66
Crawfish Pie	111
Creole Tomato and Onion Tart	11
Crispy Fried Catfish	128
Deep South, Deep-Fried Gator	133
Dee's Funeral Beans	23
Divinity Candy	65
Easy Breezy Summer Punch	31
Easy Fruit Cobbler	31
Eggplant Fritters	135
Eggplant & Shrimp Casserole	111
Elegant Crabmeat Soup	101
Fig Cake	25
German Apple Cake	13
Green Bean and Artichoke Augratin	134
Gumbo des Herbs	60
Homemade Irish Cream	30

THE RIGOLETES BRIDGE
OIL BY PHIL GALATA

Hot Sausage	123	Roasted Eggplant and Brie Soup	62
Jezebel Sauce	11	Seafood Gumbo	93
Kumquat Marmalade	27	Shrimp Pasta Salad	111
Lake Pontchartrain Crab Cakes	100	Squash Casserole	134
Limoncello	109	Sugared Pecans	47
Long Macaroni and Cheese	27	Super Grouper	129
Mandarin Orange Cake	83	The Blackwell Girls' Grits and Grillades	93
Marinated Pork Tenderloin	127	To-Die-For Crab Dip	100
Meyer Lemon Ice Box Delight	140	Tropical Island Rum Cake	42
Monkey Bread	37	Trout Amandine	115
Old Fashioned Bread Pudding with Rum Sauce	89	Turtle Soup	136
Oyster Patties	113	Vanilla Wafer Cake	24
Oysters Mosca	110		
Quick Buttermilk Biscuits	67		

Savoring Slidell

SPECIAL THANKS

FOR SHARING THEIR MEMORIES AND TALENTS

Bobbie Alexander
Sharon DeLong
John and Brenda Case
GOSH
Kay Taylor
Arriollia "Bonnie" Vanney
Gwyn Ellermann
Charlotte Lowry Collins

AND TO OUR PATRONS

Mary Bishop
Jan Brown
Juliette Hartley
Amber Thomas
Catherine Walker

STOP OF THE CAMELLIA
ACRYLIC BY KEITH DELLSPERGER